HOW TO BECOME
A POLICE OFFICER

Richard McMunn

Orders: Please contact How2become Ltd, Suite 2, 50 Churchill Square Business Centre, Kings Hill, Kent ME19 4YU. You can also order via the e mail address info@how2become.co.uk.

ISBN: 9781909229785. First published 2013

CONTENTS

INTRODUCTION

Welcome to 'How 2 Become: The insider's guide to becoming a Police Officer'. This guide has been designed to help you prepare for, and pass the tough police officer selection process.

The selection process to join the police is highly competitive. Approximately 65,000 people apply to join the police every year. But what is even more staggering is that only approximately 7,000 of those applicants will be successful. You could view this as a worrying statistic, or alternatively you could view it that you are determined to be one of the 7,000 who are successful. Armed with this insider's guide, you have certainly taken the first step to passing the police officer selection process.

The guide itself has been split up into useful sections to make it easier for you to prepare for each stage. Read each section carefully and take notes as you progress. Don't ever give up on your dreams; if you really want to become a police officer then you can do it. The way to approach the police officer selection process is to embark on a programme of 'in depth' preparation, and this guide will show you exactly how to do that.

The police officer selection process is not easy to pass, unless of course, you spend a decent amount of time preparing. Your preparation must be focused in the right areas, and also be comprehensive enough to give you every chance of success. This guide will teach you how to be a successful candidate.

The way to pass the police officer selection process is to develop your own skills and experiences around the core competencies that are required to become a police officer. Many candidates who apply to join the police will be unaware that the core competencies even exist. As you progress through this guide you will find that these important elements of the police officer role will form the foundations of your preparation. So, the first step in your preparation, and before we go any further, is to get hold of a copy of the police officer core competencies. They will usually form part of your application pack but if they don't, you can obtain a copy of them by visiting the website of the service you are applying to join.

If you need any further help with any elements of the police officer selection process, including role play, written test and interview, then we offer a wide range of products to assist you. These are all available through our online shop www.how2become.com. We also run a 1-day intensive Police Officer Course. Details are available at the website www.PoliceCourse.co.uk.

Once again, thank you for your custom and we wish you every success in your pursuit to becoming a police officer.

Work hard, stay focused and be what you want...

Best wishes,

The how2become team

The How2become Team

P.S. Attend a 1-Day police officer training course run by former police officers!

Go to www.PoliceCourse.co.uk to find out more.

PREFACE BY AUTHOR RICHARD MCMUNN

In 1993 I joined the Fire Service after serving four years in the Fleet Air Arm branch of the Royal Navy. After spending 16 successful years in the Fire Service, I decided to set up my own business and teach people like you how to prepare for a specific job. I have passed many different job applications and interviews during my life and I have also sat on the opposite side of the interview desk. Therefore, I have plenty of experience and knowledge that I will be sharing with you throughout this guide.

Throughout my career and working life I have always found that if I apply myself, and focus on the job in hand, then I will be successful. It is a formula that I have stuck with for many years, and it has always served me well. This kind of approach is one that I want to teach you over the forthcoming pages of this guide, and I hope that you will use my skills and knowledge to help you achieve the same levels of success that I have enjoyed.

Personally, I do not believe in luck when applying for jobs. I believe those candidates who successfully pass the police officer selection process do so because they thoroughly deserve it. They have prepared well and they have worked hard in order to improve their skills and knowledge.

I have always been a great believer in preparation. Preparation was my key to success, and it is also yours. Without the right level of preparation you will be setting out on the route to failure. The Police Service is very hard to join, but if you follow the steps that I have compiled within this guide then you will increase your chances of success dramatically. Remember, you are learning how to be a successful candidate, not a successful police officer!

The Police Service, like many other public services, has changed a great deal over the years and even more so in how it assesses potential candidates for police officer positions. The men and women of the UK Police Service carry out an amazing job. They are there to protect the community in which they serve and they do that job with great pride, passion and very high levels of professionalism and commitment. They are to be congratulated for the service they provide.

Before you apply to join the Police Service you need to be fully confident that you too are capable of providing that same level of service. If you think you can do it, and you can rise to the challenge, then you just might be the type of person the police are looking for.

As you progress through this guide you will notice that the core competencies required to become a police officer are a common theme. You must learn these competencies, and also be able to demonstrate throughout the selection process, if you are to have any chance of successfully passing the selection process.

Finally, I have created a short video for you that provides details about a 1-day police officer training course I am running. You will find some useful tips and hints about passing the police selection process within the video too!

Here's the video: www.PoliceCourse.co.uk

Best wishes
Richard McMunn

Attend a 1-Day
Police Officer
course run by
former Police
Officers at:
www.PoliceCourse.co.uk

CHAPTER 1

*How to pass
the Police Officer
selection process*

Before we move on to the different sections of this guide, and in particular each element of the selection process, it is important to explain to you how I intend to teach you to pass the police officer selection process.

To make it easier to explain, we will break down your preparation into the following key areas:

LEARN ABOUT THE ROLE OF A POLICE OFFICER

Before you begin to even complete the application form, it is essential that you learn about the role of a police officer. This is for a number of reasons. The first reason is that you want to be 100% certain that this job is for you. I know a few people who have joined the police only to leave a few months later because 'it wasn't what they expected'.

The second reason is that it will help you to pass the selection process. If you understand what the role of a police officer really involves, and not what you may think it involves, then you will find the selection process far easier. This is particularly true in the case of the role play/interactive exercises and also the final interview (if appropriate).

There are a number of ways that you can learn about the role of a police officer. To begin with you will find some useful information contained within this guide. Secondly, you will find plenty of information on the website of the service you are applying to join.

When reading this guide, and visiting these websites, take notes on the information you learn about the police officer role. This will enable you to gain an in-depth understanding of the role and in turn this will make the selection process far easier to pass.

Top Tip: As of 2016, local police constabularies will be able to choose which order candidates take the assessments in. After your application form, you **might** have to take an online assessment, which will act as a sifting process. This will depend upon the constabulary that you are applying to, and will likely involve a series of verbal reasoning style questions. Following this, every single successful candidate will attend the assessment centre, where you will engage in role play exercise, more verbal reasoning, maths and an interview. You may also have to take a series of written exercises, however this is once again dependant on the constabulary to which you are applying. In some cases, instead of written exercises, you will asked to provide evidence that you have a relevant qualification – such as GCSE English.

LEARN AND UNDERSTAND THE CORE COMPETENCIES

The Police Officer core competencies are the blueprint to the role of a police officer. Just as the foundation for a house to be built on must be a firm base, the core competencies are the basic skills that a police officer must be able to master if he/she is to be capable of performing the role competently.

Throughout this guide I will make continued reference to the core competencies and I cannot stress enough how important they are. During the selection process you will be assessed against the core competencies at every stage, therefore you must learn them, understand them, and most importantly be able to demonstrate them at every stage of selection, if you are to have any chance of succeeding.

It is important that you obtain a copy of the police officer core competencies prior to completing the application form. You will also use the core competencies during your preparation for the assessment centre and also the final interview, if applicable.

APPLY THE CORE COMPETENCIES TO EVERY STAGE OF SELECTION

During the preface I stated that you are learning how to be a successful candidate, not a successful police officer. Once you pass the selection process, the Police Service will train you to become a competent member of their team. During selection they are looking to see whether or not you have the potential to become a police officer and they will use the core competencies as a basis for assessment. At every stage of the process you must demonstrate the core competencies and I will show you how to achieve this within this guide.

IMPROVE YOUR FITNESS LEVELS

Surprisingly, most candidates who fail the selection process do so during the fitness tests. They concentrate so much on passing the assessment centre that they neglect the other important area of fitness. Do not settle for scraping through the fitness tests but instead look to excel. You will find that as your fitness levels increase, so will your confidence and concentration levels. This in turn will help you to pass the selection process.

I strongly believe that if you follow the simple steps above, and you apply the remainder of the information that is contained within this guide, then your chances of passing the selection process will increase tremendously.

THE POLICE OFFICER

The first step on the road to passing the police officer selection process is to learn as much as possible about the role. On the following pages you will find brief details about the role and your training. The information provided is for example purposes only and you must check with the service you are applying to join that it is relevant to you. In addition to reading and absorbing this information, I recommend you visit the website of the Police Service you are applying to join, and also the website www.policecourse.co.uk.

The great thing about the life of a police officer is that you have the ability to make a difference. On many occasions you will be able to motivate situations to change people's lives by your own actions. It is a demanding but highly satisfying career, which will provide you with the opportunity to make a difference to your community. You will be challenged daily but will have the tools and skills to be confident in your own ability to do the right thing.

Working in the Police Service is a challenging job, with many rewards. It provides the opportunity to perform a wide range of roles and to take personal responsibility for helping others. The service strives to treat everyone fairly and you should also be prepared to do the same. Dignity and respect are key elements of a police officer's working life. There is no greater feeling than bringing offenders to justice, especially if it has involved hard work, gathering information, intelligence, identifying the offender and making the arrest.

Unfortunately, for every offender there will be at least one victim and the arrest means nothing if justice in a court does not follow. In order to bring offenders to justice successfully you will need to carry out your job competently. This will mean following correct policies and procedures as well as creating accurate and concise paperwork. When all these aspects come together you know then that you've joined a very special team.

Police officers are responsible for maintaining law and order, and providing a service to the public that ensures their safety, well-being and the security of their property and possessions. Above all, they are there to serve the community and this principle is the basis of all policing policy within the UK. The police are not there to control society, but rather work with society in order to reduce crime and make the community a safe place to live.

It is important that you remember that you are there to serve the public and you don't think that life as a police officer is all about catching and convicting criminals. You must be prepared to have the community's interests at heart which is why you will be assessed against this important element during the selection process. Duties of a police officer can include patrolling on foot or in cars, investigating crime scenes or attending incidents and interacting with your community. Of course, there will be times when you need to work on the administrative side of the role and also be prepared to spend time in court giving evidence. Once again you will be assessed against this area during selection.

Being a police officer is certainly a demanding and responsible job. The rewards are that you can help prevent crime and protect the public, but policing can also frequently be emotionally taxing and challenging. You need to ensure that you are prepared for this side of the job. You might be called on to tell a mother that her daughter has been injured or killed in a road accident, or endure verbal abuse while investigating an incident. During my career in the Fire Service I attended many incidents where a member of the public had sadly lost their life. I did not envy the police officers who had the task of breaking the terrible news to the families and relatives of the victim. In order to carry out this part of the role you will need great skill, courage and sensitivity. Once again, you will be assessed against this area during the selection process. Finally, it can also be an extremely physically gruelling and demanding job. For example, you might spend five hours on the beat in extremely cold conditions. Therefore your fitness levels must be good enough to withstand the demands of the job.

More than 65,000 people apply to join the police each and every year so the competition is fierce. Only 7,000 of those applicants are usually successful so it is vital that you prepare yourself well in advance of the application process.

The most common reason that the UK Police Service turn people down is due to their lack of physical fitness. Whilst the tests are not very difficult, you must prepare well for them.

In total, there are 43 Police Services and more than 126,000 police officers in England and Wales – about one for every 400 people. In Scotland there are eight Police Services. The person in charge of each constabulary is a Chief Constable, except in London, where the Metropolitan Police and the City of London Police are each headed by a Commissioner.

As well as responding to more than six million 999 emergency calls each year, the police must contend with a vast array of crimes, from simple assaults to complex fraud.

POLICE PROBATIONARY TRAINING

Once you have successfully passed the police officer selection process you will undertake a long period of intensive training that is designed to develop you into a competent police officer. Your initial recruitment training will last about 30 weeks and it is a combination of classroom based tuition and on the job training which is carried out under the supervision of an experienced officer. Once you have spent sufficient time under supervised patrol you'll then be permitted to go out alone providing you have passed the necessary assessments and examinations.

I will now provide a more detailed breakdown of a police officer's probationary training. Please note that the following information is provided as an example only and should not be relied upon to be accurate.

THE INITIAL POLICE OFFICER TRAINING COURSE

The probationary period for student police officers lasts for two years during which time training is delivered in four distinct phases.

These phases are:

Phase 1 – Induction
In this phase, student officers are introduced to the Constabulary and important foundation areas are covered.

Phase 2 – Community Safety and Partnerships
This phase concentrates on crime and disorder, community safety and community engagement, where students will engage with community members at different times throughout the course.

Phase 3 – Supervised Patrol

This phase consists of two elements – Phase 3a is mainly classroom-based input combined with 'multi-practical' days, community engagement and some supervised patrol in Professional Development Units (PDUs). The above phases last for 22 weeks.

Phase 3b involves 10 weeks supervised patrol with tutor constables based in the PDUs.

Phase 4 – Independent Patrol
This will consist of the period from the start of independent patrol up to the point of 'confirmation' (after two years) and includes an additional 30 days continued professional development.

All training is usually now delivered within the Constabulary area. There is not normally a requirement to travel away from home for a residential course, although you should confirm this with your chosen Police Service.

OPPORTUNITIES FOR PROGRESSION

If you are good at your job and you are a motivated and ambitious person then there will certainly be many opportunities for promotion within the service.

The Police Service will always need officers on the beat, but it also needs managers who are capable of driving the service forward in the direction it requires. Everyone in the Police Service has an equal opportunity for promotion, so if you are keen and enthusiastic, then there's nothing to stop you from reaching the top!

As you are probably aware, the Police Service also operates a High Potential Development Scheme. This scheme provides fast-track opportunities for those individuals who can demonstrate the right level of potential. The Police Service promotion scheme is open to everyone and is based upon merit. Work hard and you will be rewarded!

THE WORKING WEEK

A normal working week for a Police Officer consists of 40 hours, which is usually divided up on a shift basis.

The shift pattern that you will normally work will form part of your contract and these do vary between each Police Service. All of the ranks below superintendent will be given two rest days every week and compensation will be given if you ever have to work during those two days.

If you need to know more about the different types of shift pattern you'll be required to work then you should contact your local constabulary.

COMMUNITY SAFETY PARTNERSHIPS

During my time in the Fire Service I sat on many different Community Safety Partnerships, or CSP's as they are otherwise called. In some areas these partnerships will be called an alternative name such as 'Crime and Disorder Reduction Partnerships'.

One of the main purposes of CSP's is for the local Police Service to meet up with other important organisations such as the Fire Service, Ambulance Service and the Local Authority in order to discuss ways in which they can tackle crime collectively and make the community a safer place in which to live. There are Community Safety Partnerships for nearly every local authority area in England and Wales. Each one produces an audit and strategy for its local area.

Many partnerships look into community issues relating to their own particular area and some of those issues are concerned with the reduction of crime, anti-social behaviour, graffiti and fly-tipping to name but a few.

It is far easier for local authorities (councils) to improve community safety when they work in collaboration with other stakeholders such as the Fire and Rescue Services, Social Services, The Probation Service, CCTV working groups etc. For many years Police Services and other stakeholders worked in isolation, until it was identified that more could be done if they worked with other relevant partners.

It is important to be aware that your work as a police officer may be as a direct result of requests from these partnerships. For example, there may be a problem with anti-social behaviour in a specific area of your County and you will be working hard to combat the problem.

POLICE COMMUNITY SUPPORT OFFICERS

Police community support officers (PCSOs) do not have the same powers as a fully-fledged police officer, yet they are a highly important part of crime prevention. They carry out visible patrolling within a specific area and are an effective crime deterrent, especially with regard to anti-social behaviour. Members of the public are more likely to provide PCSOs with important information relating to crime and anti-social behaviour as they spend more time in a specific area getting to know the community.

As well as being able to issue fixed penalty tickets for minor anti-social behaviour, PCSOs can also demand the name and address of a person acting in an anti-social manner. This information can then be passed on to the police so that the relevant action can be taken. Other PCSO powers include being able to confiscate alcohol being consumed in a public place, confiscate tobacco from young people who are under age, and seize any vehicles that are being used to potentially harm other people such as by joy-riders.

During your time within the service you will be required to work with PCSOs in your local area. It is important that you can work effectively other members of the Police Service, both uniformed and non-uniformed, as part of a team in order to make the community a safer place to live.

NEIGHBOURHOOD WARDENS

Neighbourhood Wardens have been introduced by the Government to provide a highly visible, uniformed, semi-official presence in residential areas, town centres and high-crime areas. Unlike police community support officers, neighbourhood wardens do not have any police powers. They are designed to be the eyes and ears of the community, looking to improve the quality of life of a specific area within the community.

As a police officer, you will be working closely with Neighbourhood Wardens and also with members of the Neighbourhood Watch scheme, utilising their information to help reduce crime and anti-social behaviour in the area that you are responsible for.

We have now covered a number of important aspects of the police officer's role. Remember that the role is highly comprehensive and it involves a lot more than simply bringing offenders to justice. During your preparation you will need to visit the website of the Police Service you are applying to join and also read your recruitment literature to gain an in-depth knowledge of the service. If I was to ask you the question "what can you tell me about the role of a police officer?" would you be able to answer it effectively?

Now let's move onto my top 10 insider tips that will assist you during your preparation for becoming a police officer.

Attend a 1-Day Police Officer course run by former Police Officers at:

www.PoliceCourse.co.uk

CHAPTER 2

The Top 10 insider tips and advice

The following 10 insider tips have been carefully put together to increase your chances of success during the police officer selection process. Therefore, it is important that you follow them carefully. Whilst some of them will appear obvious they are still important tips which you need to follow.

INSIDER TIP 1 – BE FULLY PREPARED AND FOCUSED

When you are applying for any career it is of vital importance that you prepare yourself fully for every stage of the selection process. What I mean is that you do everything you can to find out what is required of you. For example, most people do not read the guidance notes that accompany the application form, and then they wonder why they fail that particular section.

Make sure you read every bit of information you receive at least twice and understand what is required in order to pass. Things in life do not come easy and you must be prepared to work hard. Go out of your way to prepare – for example, get a friend or relative to act out a role-play scenario and see how you deal with it. When completing the application form allocate plenty of time to do it neatly, concisely and correctly. Don't leave it until the night before the closing date to fill out the form as you will be setting yourself out to fail.

I will talk about 'preparation' on many occasions throughout this guide and I want you to take on board my advice.

Break down your preparation in the following 4 key areas:

Area 1 – Learn about the role of a police officer.

Area 2 – Learn and understand the core competencies.

Area 3 – Prepare to apply the core competencies to every stage of the selection process.

Area 4 – Improve your physical fitness.

In addition to your preparation strategy, it is also very important to believe in your own abilities and take advantage of the potential that's within you. If you work hard then you will be rewarded!

Whenever you come up against hurdles or difficult situations and experiences, always try to look for the opportunity to improve yourself. For example, if you have applied for the police previously and failed, what have you done to improve your chances of success the second time around? Did you find out what areas you failed on and have you done anything to improve?

INSIDER TIP 2 – UNDERSTAND AND BELIEVE IN EQUALITY AND FAIRNESS, AND BE ABLE TO DEMONSTRATE IT DURING THE SELECTION PROCESS

Equality and fairness are crucial in today's society. We must treat each other with respect, dignity and understand that people come from different backgrounds and cultures to our own.

Treat people how you expect to be treated – with dignity and respect. If you do not believe in equality, fairness and dignity, then you are applying for the wrong job. Police officers are role models within society and people will look to you to set an example. For example, you wouldn't expect to see a police officer bullying or shouting at a member of the public in an aggressive manner would you? As a police officer you will only use force in exceptional circumstances. You will be required to use your interpersonal skills to diffuse situations and you will need to treat people fairly and equally at all times.

During the selection process your understanding and knowledge of equality and fairness issues will be tested on the application form, at the written tests and also during the interview and role-play scenarios. The core competency that relates to respect for race and diversity is the most important and you will not only have to learn it, but also believe in it.

There are many ways that you can prepare for this important core competency and within this guide I have provided you with a number of useful tips and advice that I recommend you spend time learning. Don't leave your success to chance. Make sure you understand exactly what equality and fairness and respect for race and diversity means and also what they stand for. More importantly, believe in them!

INSIDER TIP 3 – BE PHYSICALLY AND MENTALLY FIT

Being prepared, both physically and mentally, is important if you are to succeed in your application to become a police officer. Even if you only have a few weeks to prepare, there are lots of ways in which you can improve your chances of success.

Many people who successfully pass the selection process are physically fit. Being physically fit has plenty of advantages in addition to simply improving your health. For example, raised self-esteem and confidence in your appearance are also benefits to keeping fit. A person with good health and fitness generally shines when it comes to how they look, how they treat others, and how they go about their day-to-day activities.

In addition to the above, the benefits of 'fitness of mind' are equally as important when tackling the selection process. When applying to join the police you will be learning new skills and developing old ones. The fitter your mind, the easier this will be. If you are fit, both physically and mentally, then you will be able to prepare for longer. You will find that your stamina levels will increase and therefore your ability to practise and prepare will increase too.

If you prepare yourself fully for the selection process then you will feel more confident on the day, when you are under pressure. Make sure you also get plenty of sleep in the build-up to selection and ensure you eat a healthy balanced diet.

Many of us underestimate the importance of a healthy diet. The saying 'we are what we eat' makes a lot of sense and you will find that if you just spend a week or two eating and drinking the right things you will begin to look and feel healthier. Avoid junk food, alcohol and cigarettes during your preparation and your concentration levels will increase greatly, helping you to get the most out of the work you put in.

Give yourself every opportunity to succeed!

INSIDER TIP 4 – LEARN ABOUT THE POLICE SERVICE YOU ARE APPLYING TO JOIN

This is important for a number of reasons. To begin with, you may be asked a question on the application form that relates to your knowledge of the role of a police officer and also why you want to join that particular constabulary. As you can appreciate, many candidates will apply for a number of different constabularies all at once in an attempt to secure a job as a police officer. The Police Service you are applying to join wants to know what exactly attracts you to them. In order to be able to provide a good response to this type of question, you will need to carry out some research.

The second reason is that some Police Services are now holding 'final interviews', which are in addition to the standard competency based assessment centre interview. During this interview it is guaranteed that you will be asked questions relating to your knowledge of the service.

Most Police Services have a website. Visit their website and find out what they are doing in terms of community policing. Remember that the job of a police officer is not just about catching criminals. It is about delivering the best possible service to the public and responding to their needs. Understanding what the police in your area are trying to achieve will demonstrate enthusiasm, commitment and an understanding of what your job will involve if you are successful.

If you can tell the interview panel about the policing area, current crime trends and statistics, community policing issues and even diversity recruitment, then you will be displaying a far greater knowledge of their constabulary and also showing them that you have made the effort!

If you were interviewing a candidate for employment in your Police Service, what would you expect to them to know about your organisation? You would probably expect them to know great deal of information. Learn as much information as possible about the service you are applying to join and be extremely thorough in your preparation.

INSIDER TIP 5 – LEARN AND UNDERSTAND THE CORE COMPETENCIES

VERY IMPORTANT – DO NOT IGNORE

The police officer core competencies form the fundamental requirements of the role. They identify how you should perform and they are key to the role of a police officer. Read them carefully and make sure you understand them, they are crucial to your success!

Throughout the selection process you should concentrate on the core competencies, constantly trying to demonstrate them at every stage.

When completing the application form your answers should be based around the core competencies. The same rule applies to the written tests, the interview and also the role-play exercises. The most effective way to achieve this is to use 'keywords and phrases' in your responses to the application form and interview questions. You can also adopt this method when tackling the role-plays and the written tests. Using keywords and phrases that correspond to the core competencies will gain you higher scores. Within this guide I will show you how to achieve this, but the first step is for you to learn the core competencies.

Make sure you have a copy of the competencies next to you when completing the application form and whilst preparing for the assessment centre.

The core competencies cover a wide range of required skills and attributes including team working, customer focus, problem solving and equality and fairness issues, to name but a few.

This is the most important tip I can provide you with – Do not ignore it!

INSIDER TIP 6 – BE PATIENT AND LEARN FROM YOUR MISTAKES

We can all become impatient when we really want something in life but sometimes it may take us a little longer than expected to reach our goals.

Try to understand that the Police Service receives many thousands of applications each year and it takes time for them to process each one. Don't contact the Police Service with a view to chasing up your application but rather wait for them to get in touch with you. Use the time in between your results wisely, concentrating on the next stage of the selection process. For example, as soon as you submit your application form, start working on your preparation for the assessment centre. 99% of candidates will not start their preparation for the assessment centre until they receive their results. They can't be bothered to prepare for the next stage until they receive conformation that they've been successful, and as a result, they are missing out on a few extra weeks practise time.

During the police officer courses that I teach I am amazed at how many students have their assessment the following week. They sometimes inform me that they have done no preparation since prior to the course and this always baffles me. Remember that you are applying to join a job that will pay you a salary of approximately £30,000 a year! That to me is worth studying very hard for. So, use every bit of spare time you get wisely by not sitting around in between results but rather using that time to prepare for the next stage.

Once again, whilst teaching students, I am always left amazed at how many of them have previously failed selection, yet done nothing to find out why they failed and in particular which areas they need to improve on. If you have previously been through selection then it is crucial that you find out why you failed. This will allow you to improve for next time. You should receive a feedback form from the Police Service informing you which areas you need to improve on. It is pointless going through selection again unless you improve on your weak areas, as you will simply make the same mistakes again.

INSIDER TIP 7 - UNDERSTAND DIVERSITY AND THE BENEFITS IT BRINGS TO A WORKFORCE AND SOCIETY

A diverse community has great benefits and the same can be said for a diverse workforce.

The Police Service is no exception and it needs to represent the community in which it serves. It society itself is multi-cultural, then the Police Service needs to be too, if it is to provide the best possible service to the community in which it serves.

Ask yourself the question "What is diversity?" If you cannot answer it then you need to find out. You will almost certainly be asked a question about it during the application form stage and the final interview, if applicable.

The Police Service must uphold the law fairly and appropriately to protect, respect, help and reassure everyone in all communities. The Police Service must also meet all of the current legislative requirements concerning human rights, race, disability and all employment law that relates to equality.

The focus of the Police Service is to provide a service that responds to the needs of all communities, ensuring the promotion of fair working practices at all times. The concept of diversity encompasses acceptance and respect. It means understanding that each individual is unique, and recognising our individual differences. These can be along the dimensions of race, ethnicity, gender, sexual orientation, socio-economic status, age, physical abilities, religious beliefs, political beliefs, or other ideologies. It is about understanding each other and moving beyond simple tolerance to embracing and celebrating the rich dimensions of diversity contained within each individual.

Learn, understand and believe in diversity. It is important during the selection process and even more important in relation to your role as a police officer.

INSIDER TIP 8 – DO NOT GIVE UP UNTIL YOU HAVE REACHED YOUR GOAL

If you don't reach the required standard at the first or subsequent attempts, don't give up. So long as you always try to better yourself, there is always the chance that you will succeed. If you do fail any of the stages look at the area(s) you need to improve on.

Did you fail the fitness test? If so then there are ways of improving. Don't just sit back and wait for the next opportunity to come along, prepare for it straight away and you'll increase your chances for next time.

Many people give up on their goals far too easily. Learning to find the positive aspects of negative situations is a difficult thing to do but a skill that anyone can acquire through practice and determination.

If you really want to achieve your goals then anything is

possible.

During your preparation set yourself small targets each week. For example, your first week may be used to concentrate on learning the core competencies. Your second week can be used to prepare for your written responses on the application form and so on.

If you get tired or feel de-motivated at any time during your preparation, walk away from it and give yourself a break. You may find that you come back to it re-energised, more focused and determined to succeed!

INSIDER TIP 9 – PRACTICE THE ROLE-PLAY EXERCISES WITH A FRIEND OR RELATIVE

The role-play scenarios can be a daunting experience, especially if you've never done anything like this before. Whilst the Police Service will advise you to be yourself, there are ways in which you can prepare and subsequently increase your chances of success.

The way to prepare for the role-plays is to act them out in a room with a friend or relative. Within this guide you have been provided with a number of example role-play scenarios. Use these to practise with, and hone your skills in each area of the core competencies that are being assessed.

The only way that you will be able to understand what is required during the role-play exercises is to learn the assessable core competencies. For example, if you are being assessed against the core competency of customer focus, then you will need to demonstrate the following during each role-play scenario:

- Be professional and present an appropriate image in line with your brief and job description.

- Focus on the needs of the customer in every scenario.

- Sort out any problems as soon as possible and apologise for any errors or mistakes that have been made.

- Ask the customer whether they are satisfied with your actions or not. If they are not, then take alternative steps to make them satisfied if possible.

- Keep the customer updated on progress.

Doing all of the above, in addition to covering the other assessable areas, can be quite a difficult task. However, if you practise these skills regularly in the build-up to your assessment then you will find it becomes easier and easier the more that you do.

INSIDER TIP 10 – PRACTISE A MOCK INTERVIEW

Mock interviews are a fantastic way to prepare for both the assessment centre interview, and also the final interview, if applicable.

During the build-up to interviews in the past, I would write down a number of predicted interview questions that I had created during my research. I would then ask a friend or relative to ask me these questions under formal interview conditions. I found this to be excellent preparation and it certainly served me well during all of my career interviews. I would estimate that I was successful at over 90% of all interviews I attended. I put this success purely down to this form of preparation.

I would also strongly recommend that you sit down in front of a long mirror and respond to the same set of interview questions. Watch your interview technique. Do you slouch? Do you fidget and do you overuse your hands?

It is important that you work on your interview technique during the build-up to the assessment centre and the final interview.

Do not make the mistake of carrying out little or no preparation, because you can be guaranteed that some of the other candidates will have prepared fully. Make sure you put in the time and effort and practise a number of mock interviews. You will be amazed at how confident you feel during the real interview.

BONUS TIP – CONSIDER CARRYING OUT SOME COMMUNITY WORK

Demonstrating that you are capable of working effectively in the community before you join the police will give you a positive edge over other candidates. Being able to add this information to your application and also at the interview stage will make you stand out from the rest of the competition.

Why not organise a small charity event in your local area? Maybe a sponsored swim, cycle ride or car wash? The reason why I advise undertaking this type of project is that it gives you more relevant experiences to draw on during the selection process.

If you organise such an event on your own or as a team then it demonstrates your ability to organise and solve problems, which are key police officer core competencies. It also demonstrates that you are a caring person and that you are prepared to go out of your way to help others. You may also get fit in the process!

Other effective ways of working in the community are either through neighbourhood watch schemes, becoming a special constable, part-time firefighter or carrying out any form of voluntary work. Make the effort and go out on a limb to stand out from the rest of the applicants.

Now that we have taken a look at the top insider tips and advice, let us now put all that we have learnt so far into practice. The first step is the successful completion of the application form.

Attend a 1-Day Police Officer course run by former Police Officers at:

www.PoliceCourse.co.uk

CHAPTER 3

*How to complete
the Application form*

INTRODUCTION

The application form is the first stage of the selection process for becoming a police officer. During this section I will provide you with a step by step approach to completing a successful application. It is important to point out that I have used a number of the more common types of application form questions within this section and it is your responsibility to confirm that they relate to your particular form. I have deliberately not made reference to any sections of the form that relate to personal details, simply because what you write here is based on you and you alone.

Whenever I have completed application forms in the past I have always set aside plenty of time to give them justice. I would recommend you allow at least five evenings to complete the form, breaking it up into manageable sections. Many candidates will try and complete the form in one sitting and as a result their concentration will wane and so will the quality of their submission.

You will be asked a number of questions on the application form and on the following pages I have provided you with some tips and advice on how to approach these questions. Please remember that these are provided as a guide only and you should base your answers around your own experiences in both work life and personal life. Questions that are based around 'knowledge, skills and experience' are looking for you to demonstrate that you can meet the requirements of the 'person specification' for the job you are applying for. Therefore, your answer should match these as closely as possible.

Your first step is to find out what the 'person specification' is for the particular constabulary you are applying to join.

Essentially, the role of a police officer is made up of a number of core competencies. You may receive these in your application pack or alternatively they can usually be found on the website of the service you are applying to join. Whatever you do, make sure you get a copy of them, and have them by your side when completing the application form. Basically you are looking to match your responses with the police officer core competencies.

Once you have found the 'core competencies', now is the time to structure your answer around these, ensuring that you briefly cover each area based upon your own experiences in both your work life and personal life.

The core competencies that form the basis of the police officer role are similar to the following. Please note that the core competencies can, and do, change from time to time so It Is Important to confirm that they are correct.

PUBLIC SERVICE

Demonstrates a real belief in public service, focusing on what matters to the public and will best serve their interests. Understands the expectations, changing needs and concerns of different communities, and strives to address them. Builds public confidence by talking with people in local communities to explore their viewpoints and break down barriers between them and the police. Understands the impact and benefits of policing for different communities, and identifies the best way to deliver services to them. Works in partnership with other agencies to deliver the best possible overall service to the public.

OPENNESS TO CHANGE

Positive about change, adapting rapidly to different ways of working and putting effort into making them work. Flexible and open to alternative approaches to solving problems. Finds better, more cost-effective ways to do things, making suggestions for change. Takes an innovative and creative approach to solving problems.

SERVICE DELIVERY

Understands the organisation's objectives and priorities, and how own work fits into these. Plans and organises tasks effectively, taking a structured and methodical approach to achieving outcomes. Manages multiple tasks effectively by thinking things through in advance, prioritising and managing time well. Focuses on the outcomes to be achieved, working quickly and accurately and seeking guidance when appropriate.

PROFESSIONALISM

Acts with integrity, in line with the values and ethical standards of the Police Service. Takes ownership for resolving problems, demonstrating courage and resilience in dealing with difficult and potentially volatile situations. Acts on own initiative to address issues, showing a strong work ethic and demonstrating extra effort when required. Upholds professional standards, acting honestly and ethically, and challenges unprofessional conduct or discriminatory behaviour. Asks for and acts on feedback, learning from experience and developing own professional skills and knowledge. Remains calm and professional under pressure, defusing conflict and being prepared to step forward and take control when required.

DECISION MAKING

Gathers, verifies and assesses all appropriate and available information to gain an accurate understanding of situations. Considers a range of possible options before making clear, timely, justifiable decisions. Reviews decisions in the light of new information and changing circumstances. Balances risks, costs and benefits, thinking about the wider impact of decisions. Exercises discretion and applies professional judgement, ensuring actions and decisions are proportionate and in the public interest.

WORKING WITH OTHERS

Works co-operatively with others to get things done, willingly giving help and support to colleagues. Is approachable, developing positive working relationships. Explains things well, focusing on the key points and talking to people using language they understand. Listens carefully and asks questions to clarify understanding, expressing own views positively and constructively. Persuades people by stressing the benefits of a particular approach, keeps them informed of progress and manages their expectations. Is courteous, polite and considerate, showing empathy and compassion. Deals with people as individuals and addresses their specific needs and concerns. Treats people with respect and dignity, dealing with them fairly and without prejudice regardless of their background or circumstances.

Now that we have taken a brief look at the core competencies, we can start to look at some of the application form questions. But before we do this, take a read of the following important tips, which will help you to submit a first class application.

- Make sure you read the whole of the application form at least twice before preparing your responses, including the guidance notes.

- Read and understand the person specification and the police officer core competencies.

- Try to tailor your answers around the 'core competencies' and include any keywords or phrases you think are relevant.

- Make sure you base your answers on actual events that you have experienced either in your work life or personal life.

- Fill the form out in the correct ink colour. If you fail to follow this simple instruction then your form may end up in the bin!

- If there is a specific word count for each question, make sure you stick to it.

- Do not lie.

- Get someone to read your practice/completed application form to check for spelling/grammar mistakes. You lose marks for poor grammar/spelling.

- Answer all of the questions to the best of your ability. If you leave a question blank, it is highly unlikely you will move on to the next stage.

- Follow the prompts given in each question. They will help to give your answers a clearer structure.

- Use examples from your work, social, domestic or educational life to answer the questions. In these examples, they are looking for evidence of specific behaviours which research has shown to be essential to police work.

- Be specific: they want to know what YOU said or did on a given occasion to deal with the situation. It's therefore important that the examples you provide are your own experiences and as detailed as possible.

- Try to use examples that you found difficult or challenging to deal with. These answers tend to achieve better marks.

- Write clearly and concisely. They expect your answers to be focused, succinct and fluently written, as any police report or statement would need to be. This means writing in complete sentences rather than notes or bullet points.

- Pay attention to your handwriting, spelling, punctuation and grammar. Remember this is a formal application so the use of jargon and slang is unacceptable.

- Do not add extra sheets, write outside the space provided or write between the lines. No marks will be given for evidence outside the space provided.

- Finally, send your application form recorded delivery. This will prevent your form going missing in the post, which happens more often that you think.

SAMPLE APPLICATION FORM QUESTIONS AND RESPONSES

The following sample application form questions may not be applicable to your specific form. However, they will provide you with some excellent tips and advice on how to approach the questions.

SAMPLE QUESTION NUMBER 1

What knowledge, skills and experiences do you have that will enable you to meet the requirements of a police officer?

ANSWER (EXAMPLE ONLY)

"In my previous employment as a customer services assistant I was required to work closely with the general public on many occasions. Often I would be required to provide varied solutions to customers' problems or complaints after listening to their concerns. It was always important for me to listen carefully to what they had to say and respond in a manner that was both respectful and understanding.

On some occasions I would have to communicate with members of the public from a different race or background and I made sure I paid particular attention to making sure they understood how I was going to resolve their problems. I would always be sensitive to how they may have been feeling on the other end of the telephone.

Every Monday morning the team that I was a part of would hold a meeting to discuss ways in which we could improve our service to the customer. During these meetings I would always ensure that I contributed and shared any relevant experiences I had during the previous week. Sometimes during the group discussions I would find that some members of the group were shy and not very confident at coming forward, so I always sensitively tried to involve them wherever possible.

I remember on one occasion during a meeting I provided a solution to a problem that had been on-going for some time. I had noticed that customers would often call back to see if their complaint had been resolved, which was often time-consuming for the company to deal with. So I suggested that we should have a system where customers were called back after 48 hours with an update of progress in relation to their complaint. My suggestion was taken forward and is now an integral part of the company's procedures. I found it quite hard at first to persuade managers to take on my idea but I was confident that the change would provide a better service to the public we were serving."

First of all read the example answer we have provided above. Then try to 'match' the answer to the core competencies that are relevant to the role of a police officer and you will begin to understand what is required.

For example, the first paragraph reads as follows:

"In my previous employment as a customer services assistant I was required to work closely with the general public on many occasions. Often I would be required to provide varied solutions to customers' problems or complaints after listening to their concerns. It was always important for me to listen carefully to what they had to say and respond in a manner that was both respectful and understanding."

The above paragraph matches elements of the core competency of Public Service.

Now take a look at the next paragraph:

"On some occasions I would have to communicate with members of the public from a different race or background and I made sure I paid particular attention to making sure they understood how I was going to resolve their problems for them. I would always be sensitive to how they may have been feeling on the other end of the telephone."

The response matches elements of the core competency of Working with Others.

Hopefully you are now beginning to understand what is required and how important it is to 'match' your response with the core competencies that are being assessed. Remember to make sure you read fully the guidance notes that are contained within your application pack. You will also hopefully start to realise why I recommend you set aside five evenings to complete the form!

It is also possible to use examples from your personal life, so don't just think about work experiences but look at other aspects of your life too. Try also to think of any community work that you have been involved in. Have you been a special constable or do you work for a charity or other similar organisation? Maybe you are a member of neighbourhood watch and if so you should find it quite a simple process to match the core competencies.

Try to tailor your responses to the core competencies that are being assessed and briefly cover each assessable area if possible. You may also want to try to include keywords and phrases from the core competencies when constructing your response.

I have now provided a number of sample keywords and phrases that are relevant to each core competency. These will help you to understand exactly what I mean when I say 'match' the core competencies in each of your responses.

Keywords and phrases to consider using in your responses to the application form questions and other elements of the police officer selection process.

Public Service

- Focused on the customer at all times to ensure I delivered an excellent service.

- I addressed the needs of the person I was dealing with.

- I listened to their viewpoint.

- By speaking with them I was able to build their confidence in my abilities.

- I took the time to identify the best way to meet their needs.

- I worked alongside other people to ensure the best service was delivered.

Openness to change

- I was positive about the pending change.

- I took steps to adapt to the new working-practices.

- I put in extra effort to make the changes work.

- I was flexible in my approach to work.

- I searched for alternative ways to deal with the situation.

- I took an innovative approach to working with the new guidelines and procedures.

Service delivery

- I consider the organisations main objectives and aims whilst carrying out my work.

- Used an action plan to help me achieve the task.

- I was organised in my approach to the working situation.

- I managed a number of different tasks at once and ensured that my time-management was effective.

- I focused at all times on the end result.

- I asked for clarification whenever I was unsure.

Professionalism

- I acted at all times in a professional and ethical manner.

- I took responsibility for solving the problem.

- I stood by my decision despite the objections from others.

- I remained calm at all times and in control of the situation.

- I immediately challenged the inappropriate behaviour.

- In order to improve my performance I sought feedback from my manager.

- I took steps to defuse the conflict.

- I took control of the situation in order to achieve a positive outcome.

Decision Making

- I gathered all of the information available before making my decision.

- I verified that the information was accurate before using it to make a decision.

- I considered all possible options first.

- I reviewed my decision once the new information had become available.

- I considered the wider implications before making my decision.

- I remained impartial at all times.

- I considered the confidentiality of the information I was receiving.

Working with others

- I worked with the other members of the team to get the task completed.

- At all times I considered the other members of the team and offered my support whenever possible.

- I took steps to develop a positive working relationship with the other members of the team.

- I fully briefed the other members of the team on what we need to achieve.

- I adapted my style of communication to fit the audience.

- I listened to the other persons views and took them into consideration.

- I took positive steps to persuade the team to follow my course of action.

- I kept the others updated of my progress at all times.

- I addressed their needs and concerns immediately.

- At all times I treated the other with respect and dignity.

You will notice that I have used the word 'I' many times during the above sample keywords and phrases; this is deliberate. Remember, it is important that you explain what YOU did during your responses.

Now let's move on to some more sample application form interview questions and responses.

SAMPLE QUESTION NUMBER 2

Why have you applied for this post and what do you have to offer?

Some Police Service application forms may ask you questions based around the question above. If so, then you need to answer again in conjunction with the 'person spec' relevant to that particular constabulary.

An example answer for the above question could be based around the following:

"I believe my personal qualities and attributes would be suited to that of a police officer within this Constabulary. I enjoy working in a diverse organisation that offers many and varied challenges. I would enjoy the challenge of working in a public service environment that requires a high level of personal responsibility, openness to change and working with others. I have a high level of commitment, motivation and integrity, which I believe would help the Police Service respond to the needs of their community."

Top tips

- The length of response that you provide should be dictated by the amount of space available to you on the application form or the specified number of maximum words.

- The form itself may provide you with the facility to attach a separate sheet if necessary. If it doesn't then make sure you keep to the space provided.

- The best tip I can give you is to write down your answer first in rough before committing your answer to paper on the actual application form. This will allow you to iron out any mistakes.

SAMPLE QUESTION NUMBER 3

It is essential that police officers are capable of showing respect for other people regardless of their background. Please describe a situation when you have challenged someone's behaviour that was bullying, discriminatory or insensitive. You will be assessed on how positively you acted during the situation, and also on how well you understood what had occurred.

PART 1 – Describe the situation and also tell us about the other person or people who were involved.

"Whilst working as a sales person for my previous employer, I was serving a lady who was from an ethnic background. I was helping her to choose a gift for her son's 7th birthday when a group of four youths entered the shop and began looking around at the goods we had for sale.

For some strange reason they began to make racist jokes and comments to the lady. I was naturally offended by the comments and was concerned for the lady to whom these comments were directed.

Any form of bullying and harassment is not welcome in any situation and I was determined to stop it immediately and protect the lady from any more harm."

Top tip

- Try to answer this type of question focusing on the positive action that you took, identifying that you understood the situation. Don't forget to include keywords and phrases in your response that are relevant to the competencies that are being assessed.

- Make sure you are honest in your responses. The situations you provide MUST be real and ones that you took part in.

PART 2 – What did you say and what did you do?

"The lady was clearly upset by their actions and I too found them both offensive and insensitive. I decided to take immediate action and stood between the lady and the youths to try to protect her from any more verbal abuse or comments. I told them in a calm manner that their comments were not welcome and would not be tolerated. I then called over my manager for assistance and asked him to call the police before asking the four youths to leave the shop.

I wanted to diffuse the situation as soon as possible, being constantly aware of the lady's feelings. I was confident that the shop's CCTV cameras would have picked up the four offending youths and that the police would be able to deal with the situation.

After the youths had left the shop I sat the lady down and made her a cup of tea whilst we waited for the police to arrive. I did everything that I could to support and comfort the lady and told her that I would be prepared to act as a witness to the bullying and harassment that I had just witnessed."

Top tip

- Remember to read the core competencies before constructing your response. What are the police looking for in relation to what YOU say to others and how you act?

PART 3 – Why do you think the other people behaved as they did?

"I believe it is predominantly down to a lack of understanding, education and awareness. Unless people are educated and understand why these comments are not acceptable then they are not open to change.

They behave in this manner because they are unaware of how dangerous their comments and actions are. They believe it is socially acceptable to act this way when it certainly isn't."

Top tip

- When describing your thoughts or opinions on how others acted in a given situation, keep your personal views separate. Try to provide a response that shows a mature understanding of the situation.

PART 4 – What would have been the consequences if you had not acted as you did?

"The consequences are numerous. To begin with I would have been condoning this type of behaviour and missing an opportunity to let the offenders know that their actions are wrong (educating them). I would have also been letting the lady down, which would have in turn made her feel frightened, hurt and not supported.

We all have the opportunity to help stop discriminatory behaviour and providing we ourselves are not in any physical danger then we should take positive action to stop it."

Top tip

Try to demonstrate an understanding of what would have possibly happened if you had failed to take action.

SAMPLE QUESTION NUMBER 4

Police officers are required to work in teams and therefore they must be able to work well with others. Please describe a situation when it was necessary to work with other people in order to get something done and achieve a positive result. During this question you will be assessed on how you co-operated with the other members of the team in completing the task in hand.

PART 1 – Tell us what had to be done.

"Whilst driving along the motorway I noticed that an accident had just occurred up in front of me. Two cars were involved in the accident and some people in the car appeared to be injured. There were a number of people

stood around looking at the crash and I was concerned that help had not been called.

We needed to work as a team to call the emergency services, look after the injured people in the cars and try to stay as safe as possible."

Top tip

- Make sure you provide a response to the questions that is specific in nature. Do not fall into the trap of telling them what you 'would do' if the situation was to occur. Tell them what you DID do.

PART 2 – How was it that you became involved?

"I became involved through pure instinct. I'm not the type of person to sit in the background and let others resolve situations. I prefer to try to help out where I can and I believed that, in this situation, something needed to be done. It was apparent that people were hurt and the emergency services had not been called yet.

There were plenty of people around but they weren't working as a team to get the essentials done."

Top tip

- It is better to say that you volunteered to get involved rather than that you were asked.

PART 3 – What did you do and what did others do?

"I immediately shouted out loud and asked if anybody was a trained first aid person, nurse or doctor. A man came running over and told me that he worked for the British Red Cross and that he had a first aid kit in his car. He told

me that he would look after the injured people but that he would need an assistant. I asked a lady if she would help him and she said that she would. I then decided that I needed to call the emergency services and went to use my mobile phone.

At this point a man pointed out to me that if I used the orange emergency phone it would get through quicker and the operator would be able to locate exactly where the accident was. I asked him if he would call the emergency services on the orange phone, as he appeared to know exactly what he was doing. I noticed a lady sat on the embankment next to the hard shoulder crying and she appeared to be a bit shocked.

I asked an onlooker if he would mind sitting with her and talking to her until the ambulance got there. I thought this was important so that she felt supported and not alone.

Once that was done, the remaining onlookers and I decided to work as a team to remove the debris lying in the road, which would hinder the route for the oncoming emergency service vehicles."

Top tip

- Provide a response that is both concise and flows in a logical sequence.

PART 4 – How was it decided which way things were to be done?

"I decided to take the initiative and get everyone working as a team. I asked the people to let me know what their particular strengths were. One person was first aid trained and so he had the task of attending to the injured.

Everyone agreed that we needed to work together as a team in order to achieve the task."

PART 5 – What did you do to ensure the team were able to get the result they wanted?

"I took control of a deteriorating situation and got everybody who was stood around doing nothing involved. I made sure I asked if anybody was skilled in certain areas such as first aid and used the people who had experience, such as the man who knew about the orange emergency telephones.

I also kept talking to everybody and asking them if they were OK and happy with what they were doing. I tried my best to co-ordinate the people with jobs that I felt needed to be done as a priority."

Top tip

- Try to include details that demonstrate how your actions had a positive impact on the result.

PART 6 – What benefit did you see for yourself in what you did?

"The benefit overall was for the injured people, ensuring that they received treatment as soon as possible. However, I did feel a sense of achievement that the team had worked well together even though we had never met each other before. I also learnt a tremendous amount from the experience.

At the end we all shook hands and talked briefly and there was a common sense of achievement amongst everybody that we had done something positive. Without each other we wouldn't have been able to get the job done."

Top tip

- Try to explain that the benefit was positive.

SAMPLE QUESTION NUMBER 5

During very difficult circumstances, police officers must be able to remain calm and act logically and decisively. Please describe a situation when you have been in a very challenging or difficult situation and had to make a decision where other people disagreed with you. You will be assessed in this question on how positively you reacted in the face of adversity and challenge.

PART 1 – Tell us about the situation and why you felt it was difficult.

"Whilst working in my current position as a sales person I was the duty manager for the day as my manager had gone sick. It was the week before Christmas and the shop was very busy.

During the day the fire alarm went off and I started to ask everybody to evacuate the shop, which is our company policy. The alarm has gone off in the past but the normal manager usually lets people stay in the shop whilst he finds out if it's a false alarm.

This was a difficult situation because the shop was very busy, nobody wanted to leave and my shop assistants were disagreeing with me in my decision to evacuate the shop. Some of the customers were becoming irate as they were in the changing rooms at the time."

Top tip

- For questions of this nature you will need to focus on the core competency that relates to professionalism.

Remember to use keywords and phrases in your responses that match the core competencies being assessed.

PART 2 – Who disagreed with you and what did they say or do?

"Both the customers and my shop assistants were disagreeing with me. The customers were saying that it was appalling that they had to evacuate the shop and that they would complain to the head office about it.

The sales staff were trying to persuade me to keep everybody inside the shop and saying that it was most probably a false alarm as usual. I was determined to evacuate everybody from the shop for safety reasons and would not allow anybody to deter me from my aim.

The safety of my staff and customers was at the forefront of my mind even though it wasn't at theirs."

Top tip

- Do not become aggressive or confrontational when dealing with people who disagree with you. Remain calm at all times but be resilient in your actions if it is right to do so.

PART 3 – What did you say or do?

"Whilst remaining calm and in control I shouted at the top of my voice that everybody was to leave, even though the sound of the alarm was reducing the impact of my voice. I then had to instruct my staff to walk around the shop and tell everybody to leave whilst we investigated the problem.

I had to inform one member of staff that disciplinary action would be taken against him if he did not co-operate. Eventually, after I kept persisting, everybody began to leave the shop. I then went outside with my members of staff, took a roll call and awaited the Fire Brigade to arrive."

Top tip

- Remember to be in control at all times and remain calm. These are qualities that good police officers will possess.

PART 4 – Tell us how this situation made you feel initially.

"At first I felt a little apprehensive and under pressure but determined not to move from my position as I knew 100% that it was the right one. I was disappointed that my staff did not initially help me but the more I persisted the more confident I became.

This was the first time I had been the manager of the shop so I felt that this situation tested my courage and determination. By remaining calm I was able to deal with the situation far more effectively."

Top tip

- Do not say that you felt angry and do not use words that are confrontational.

- By staying calm you will be able to deal with situations far more effectively.

PART 5 – How did you feel immediately after the incident?

"I felt good because I had achieved my aim and I had stood by my decision. It made me feel confident that I could

do it again and deal with any difficult situation. I now felt that I had the courage to manage the shop better and had proven to myself that I was capable of dealing with difficult situations.

I had learnt that staying calm under pressure improves your chances of a successful outcome dramatically."

SAMPLE QUESTION NUMBER 6

Police Officers must deliver an excellent service to the public. It is also important that they build good working relationships with the public and other stakeholders. Describe a situation when you had to deal with someone who was disappointed with the level of service they received. Try to use an occasion where you had contact with that person over a period of time or on a number of different occasions in order to rectify the problem.

PART 1 – Describe the situation and why you think the person was not happy.

"Whilst working as a sales person in my current job, I was approached by an unhappy customer. He explained to me, in an angry manner, that he had bought a pair of running trainers for his daughter's birthday the week before. When she unwrapped her present the morning of her birthday she noticed that one of the training shoes was a size 6 whilst the other one was a size 7.

Understandably he was not happy with the level of service that he had received from our company. The reason for his dissatisfaction was that his daughter had been let down on her birthday and as a consequence he then had to travel back into town to sort out a problem that should not have occurred in the first place."

Top tip

- In order to respond to this type of question accurately you will need to study and understand the core competency that relates to public service.

- Make sure you answer the question in two parts. Describe the situation and then explain why the person was not happy.

PART 2 – Explain what you did in response to his concerns.

"Immediately I tried to diffuse his anger by telling him that I fully understood his situation and that I would feel exactly the same if I was in his position. I promised him that I would resolve the situation and offered him a cup of tea or coffee whilst he waited for me to address the problem. This appeared to have the effect of calming him down and the tone in his voice became friendlier.

I then spoke to my manager and explained the situation to him. I suggested that maybe it would be a good idea to replace the running shoes with a new pair (both the same size) and also refund the gentleman in full as a gesture to try to make up for our mistake. The manager agreed to my suggestion and so I returned to the gentleman concerned and explained what we proposed to do for him. He was delighted with the good will offer and appeared to calm down totally.

We then went over to the checkout to refund his payment and replace the running shoes. At this point I took down the gentleman's address and telephone number, which is company policy for any goods returned for refund or exchange. The man then left the shop happy with the service he had received.

The following day I telephoned the gentleman at home to check that everything was OK with the running shoes and he told me that his daughter was delighted. He also informed me that despite the initial bad experience he would still use our shop in the future."

Top tip

- Remember that public service is an important element of the role of a police officer. You must focus on the needs of the customer or the person you are dealing with at all times.

PART 3 – How did you know that the person was happy with what you did?

"I could detect a change in his behaviour as soon as I explained that I sympathised with his situation. Again, when I offered him a cup of tea or coffee I detected a change in his behaviour once more.

The tone in his voice became less agitated and angry so I took advantage of this situation and tried even harder to turn his bad experience with us into a positive one. When we offered him the refund along with the replacement of the running shoes his attitude changed again but this time he appeared to be satisfied.

Finally, when I telephoned him the following day he was so happy that he said he would come back to us again despite the initial poor level of service."

Top tip

- In your response to this part of the question try to indicate that you followed up your actions by contacting the person to see if they were satisfied with what you did for them.

PART 4 – If you hadn't acted like you did what do you think the outcome would have been?

"To begin with I believe the situation would have become even more heated and possibly untenable. His anger or dissatisfaction could have escalated if my attempts to diffuse the situation had not taken place. I also believe that we would have lost a customer and therefore lost future profits and custom for the company. There would have been a high possibility that the gentleman would have taken his complaint higher, either to our head office, trading standards or the local newspaper.

Customer service is important and we need to do everything we can (within reason) to make the level of service we provide as high as possible. I also believe that our reputation could have been damaged as that particular gentleman could have told friends or colleagues not to use our shop in the future, whereas now, he is maybe more inclined to promote us in a positive light instead."

Top tip

- Demonstrate that you have a clear understanding of what would have happened if you had not acted as you did.

- Study the core competency that is relevant to public service before answering this question.

- Use keywords and phrases in your response from the core competency that is being assessed.

SAMPLE QUESTION NUMBER 7

Police officers must be organised and manage their own time effectively. Please describe a situation when you were under pressure to carry out a number of tasks at the same time.

Tell us what you had to do, which things were a priority and why.

"Whilst working for a sales company as a manager I had 4 important tasks to complete on the last working day of every month. These tasks included stocktaking reports, approving and submitting the sales reps' mileage claims, auditing the previous month's accounts and planning the strategy for the following month's activity.

My first priority was always to approve and submit the sales reps' mileage claims. If I did not get this right or failed to get them submitted on time the reps would be out of pocket when they received their payslip. This would in turn affect morale and productivity within the office. The second task to complete would be the stocktaking reports.

This was important to complete on time as if I missed the deadline we would not have sufficient stock for the following month and therefore there would be nothing to sell and customers would not receive their goods on time. The third task would be the strategy for the following month. This was usually a simple task but still important as it would set out my plan for the following month's activities.

Finally I would audit the accounts. The reason why I would leave this task until the end is that they did not have to be submitted to Head Office until the 14th day of the month and therefore I had extra time to complete this task and ensure that I got it right the first time."

Top tip

- Try to demonstrate that you have excellent organisation skills and that you can cope with the demands and pressures of the job.

SAMPLE QUESTION NUMBER 8

Police officers must be capable of communicating effectively with lots of different people, both verbally and in writing.

Please explain a situation when you had to tell an individual or a group of people something that they may have found difficult or distressing. You will be assessed on how well you delivered the message and also on what you took into account when speaking to them.

PART 1 – Who were the people and what did you have to tell them?

"The people involved were my elderly next door neighbours. They had a cat that they had looked after for years and they were very fond of it. I had to inform them that their cat had just been run over by a car in the road."

PART 2 – Why do you think they may have found the message difficult or distressing?

"I was fully aware of how much they loved their cat and I could understand that the message I was about to tell them would have been deeply distressing. They had cherished the cat for years and to suddenly lose it would have been a great shock to them."

PART 3 – How did you deliver the message?

"To begin with I knocked at their door and ask calmly if I could come in to speak to them. Before I broke the news to them I made them a cup of tea and sat them down in a quiet room away from any distractions. I then carefully and sensitively told them that their cat had passed away following an accident in the road. At all times I took into account their feelings and I made sure I delivered the message sensitively and in a caring manner."

PART 4 – Before you delivered your message, what did you take into account?

"I took into account where and when I was going to deliver the message. It was important to tell them in a quiet room away from any distractions so that they could grieve in peace. I also took into account the tone in which I delivered the message and I also made sure that I was sensitive to their feelings. I also made sure that I would be available to support them after I had broken the news."

Top tip

- Read the question carefully and make sure you answer every element of it.

You may find on the application form that some of the questions are based around different core competencies. If this is the case then simply apply the same process of trying to match the core competencies by using keywords and phrases in your responses.

QUESTIONS BASED AROUND YOUR REASONS AND MOTIVATIONS FOR WANTING TO BECOME A POLICE OFFICER

In addition to the standard core competency based questions, you may be asked additional questions that are centred around your motivations for wanting to become a police officer with this particular Police Service.

On the following pages I have provided a number of different questions and sample responses to assist you. Please remember that the responses provided here, and in other parts of this guide, are for guidance purposes only. The responses you provide on your application form must be based around your own individual circumstances, beliefs and circumstances.

SAMPLE QUESTION NUMBER 1

How long have you been thinking about becoming a police officer and what has attracted your attention to the role?

"I have been considering a career as a police officer ever since I started my current sales manager job approximately 7 years ago. I enjoy working in a customer-focused environment and thrive on providing high levels of service to customers. I have always been aware that the police officer's role is demanding, hard work and highly challenging but the rewards of such a job are what attracted my attention in the first place.

The opportunity to work as part of an efficient team and work towards providing the community with an effective service would be highly rewarding and satisfying."

Top tip

- It is not advisable to state that you have only just become interested recently. Candidates who have been seriously thinking about the job for a while will potentially score higher marks.

- Try to demonstrate in your response that you have studied the role carefully and that you believe your skills are suited to being a police officer.

- Those candidates who state that they are attracted solely to the 'catching criminals' side of the role will not score high.

- Read the core competencies and the job description carefully before responding to this question.

- Never be critical of a previous employer.

SAMPLE QUESTION NUMBER 2

What have you done to prepare for this application?

"I have carried out a great deal of research to ascertain whether I am suitable for the role of a police officer and also to find out whether this career would suit my career aspirations. I have studied in depth the police officer core competencies to ensure that I can meet the expectations of this Police Service. I have also carried out extensive research before applying to this particular Police Service as opposed to just applying to any constabulary and hoping that I just get in.

My research began on the Internet through the official police service websites, before finally studying this particular constabulary"s website. I have also spoken to current serving police officers at my local station to ask about the role of a working police officer and how it affects their social life.

Finally, I have discussed my intentions with my immediate family to ensure that I have their full support and encouragement."

Top tip

- You will recall at the beginning of this guide how much emphasis I placed on preparation leading to success. The police want to know how much preparation you have done and also the type of preparation. If you have carried out plenty of in depth and meaningful preparation then it demonstrates to them that you are very serious about wanting this job. Those applicants who carry out little or no preparation may be simply 'going through the motions'.

FINAL TIPS FOR COMPLETING A SUCCESSFUL APPLICATION FORM

Whilst some of the following tips have already been provided within this section, it is important that we provide them again. Your success very much depends on your ability to do the following:

- Read the application form and the guidance notes at least twice before you complete it.

- If possible, photocopy the application form and complete a draft copy first. This will allow you to make any errors or mistakes without being penalised.

- Obtain a copy of the core competencies and have them at your side when completing the form.

- Take your time when completing the form and set aside plenty of time for each question. I recommend that you spend five evenings completing the application form breaking it down into manageable portions. This will allow you to maintain high levels of concentration.

- Complete the form in the correct colour ink and follow all instructions very carefully. Your form could be thrown out for simply failing to follow simple instructions.

- Be honest when completing the form and if you are unsure about anything contact the Police Service for confirmation.

- Try not to make any spelling or grammar errors. You WILL lose marks for poor spelling, grammar and punctuation.

- Try to use keywords and phrases in your responses to the assessable questions that are relevant to the core competencies.

- Get someone to check over your form for errors before you submit it. If they can't read your application form, the assessor probably won't be able to either.

- Take a photocopy of your final completed form before submitting it.

- Try to submit the form well before the closing date. Some constabularies may operate a cut-off point in terms of the number of applications they receive.

- Some forms do get lost in the post so it is advisable that you send it by recorded delivery for peace of mind.

- If your form is unsuccessful ask for feedback, if available. It is important that you learn from your mistakes.

WHAT HAPPENS AFTER I HAVE SENT OFF MY APPLICATION FORM?

Once you have completed and sent off your application form there will be a wait period before you find out whether or not you have been successful. Some constabularies will only write to you if you have been successful.

Regardless of the above, it is crucial that you start preparing for the assessment centre even before you receive your result. By starting your preparation early you will effectively be giving yourself a 2-3 week advantage over the other applicants. 99% of applicants will wait to receive their result before they start to prepare. This is where you can gain an advantage.

During the next section you will learn about the assessment centre and the different stages that you may have to go through. Prepare fully for each stage and really go out of your way to improve your skills and knowledge of the selection process.

Please note that the information you are about to read may differ between constabularies. Make sure you confirm the exact requirements of your particular assessment centre before you start preparing.

CHAPTER 4

How to pass the National Recruitment Assessment Centre

Once you have successfully passed the application form stage of the process you will be invited to attend an assessment centre. The assessment centre location will vary between constabularies but you will be provided with details, times and location. Make sure you know exactly where your venue is and don't be late.

The assessment centre is designed to assess your suitability for recruitment into the Police Service. The assessment centre is usually conducted over a period of five hours but this may vary between constabularies.

For the assessment centre you will be required to take a number of important documents with you to confirm your identification to the police. The forms of identification can vary but the more common types include:

- A full 10-year passport or TWO of the following:

- British Driving Licence;

- P45;

- Birth Certificate, issued within six weeks of birth;

- Cheque Book and Bank Card with three statements and proof of signature;

- Card containing a photograph of yourself;

- Proof of residence, e.g. Council Tax, Gas, Electricity, Water or Telephone Bill.

Make sure that you read the information given to you and take along the relevant documents as if you do not, then you won't be able to continue with the day. At the assessment centre you will be required to undertake a numerical ability test, a verbal ability test, written exercises, interactive/role-play exercises and a competency based structured interview.

Some Police Services now require you to sit a final interview which normally comes after the assessment centre.

In the numerical ability test they will ask you to answer multiple-choice questions which will measure your ability to use numbers in a rational way, correctly identifying logical relationships between numbers and, drawing conclusions and inference from them. The numerical ability test will last for 23 minutes and there are 21 questions in the test. The test will not assess simple numerical checking ability. You will be presented with a series of graphs and tables, each followed by several questions. You must choose the correct answer from a maximum of four possible answers, filling in the appropriate space on an answer sheet they will provide. The questions will require you to utilise the following numerical operations:

- Addition

- Subtraction

- Multiplication

- Division

- Averages (mean)

- Percentages

- Ratios

- Interpretation of numbers represented graphically

You will take the test in an exercise room along with the other candidates in your group. You can use a calculator for this test which will be provided for you at the assessment centre. You are not permitted to use your own calculator during this test. They will give you full instructions before you start the test.

In the verbal ability test they will ask you to answer multiple-choice questions which will measure your ability to make sense of a situation when you are given specific written information about it. The verbal ability test will last for 30 minutes and there are 28 questions in the test. Again, you will take the test in an exercise room along with the other candidates in your group. The test is split into two sections as follows —

Section A of this test has three possible answers where only ONE of which is correct, whereas Section B has four possible answers of which only ONE is correct.

In Section A they will give you a number of conclusions which you might come to. You must look at each conclusion and work out if:

A the conclusion is true given the situation described and the facts known about it;

B the conclusion is false given the situation described and the facts known about it;

Or

C it is impossible to say whether the conclusion is true or false given the situation described and the facts known about it.

In **Section B** they will give you four statements and you will be required to evaluate which ONE of the four statements is the best answer, given the information provided. Once you have made your decision you will then fill in the appropriate space on an answer sheet they provide. They will give you full instructions before you start the test.

In the written and interactive exercises, you may have to assume the role of a newly appointed customer services officer at a fictitious retail and leisure complex. You will note that the title 'customer services officer' is very similar to the role of a police officer in as much as you will be dealing with members of the public.

During the interview you may be asked questions about how you have dealt with situations in your past and I have provided you with in depth information to help you pass this stage in a separate section of this guide.

Prior to the assessment centre you will be provided with an information pack, which you must read and familiarise yourself with all of its content.

HOW TO PREPARE FOR THE ASSESSMENT CENTRE

When preparing to complete the application form you will have already learnt a considerable amount of job specific information that is relevant to the role of a police officer. Once again, the core competencies are going to form the basis of your preparation and you should have a copy of them next to you when preparing for each stage of the assessment centre.

In relation to the written tests preparation, only you will know your current skill level and will therefore need to decide how much time you allocate to this area. The majority of candidates are not overly concerned about the numerical and verbal ability tests but they are when it comes to report writing. Within this guide you will receive some invaluable advice relating to every area of assessment so make sure you read it carefully and try out the sample test questions.

The role-play exercises can be a daunting experience. However, if you practise them beforehand, and learn how to demonstrate the core competencies being assessed, then your confidence will increase dramatically. A thorough explanation of how to prepare for them has been provided within this guide. Once again, centre your role-play preparation around the core competencies, as this is how the police will assess you.

In addition to the assessment centre interview, many Police Services have introduced a 'final interview' as I have already mentioned. The reason for this additional interview is so that the Police Service can assess you in addition to the competency based structured interview which involves set questions.

The assessment centre interview focuses purely on the core competencies and, providing you put in the work, it is relatively easy to pass. Within this guide I have provided you with detailed information on how to prepare for both types of interview. It is important that you check with the service you are applying to join whether or not you will be required to sit a final interview.

I will now break down each assessment centre area in detail to allow you to prepare effectively.

THE WRITTEN TESTS

When preparing for the numerical and verbal ability tests, the most effective way to increase your scores is to simply practice plenty of sample questions. Within this section I have provided you with a number of sample test questions. In addition to these you may also decide to purchase additional testing resources. If you do decide to pursue this option then I recommend the following:

1. Numerical reasoning and verbal reasoning testing booklets from the website www.how2become.com.

2. Consider practicing online tests through my website www.how2become.com.

3. You can also obtain many books for the police selection process by searching for 'how2become' at Amazon.co.uk.

I have now provided you with a number of practice sample questions that you may encounter during your tests. It is unlikely that you will be asked these exact questions during your assessment, but please do use them as part of your preparation.

Work as quickly as possible through each question and see how well you score. Try to understand each question and read it carefully. The answers to each question are at the end of the exercises.

Use a pen and paper, and answer each question as **TRUE**, **FALSE** or **IMPOSSIBLE TO SAY**.

REMEMBER TO ANSWER YOUR QUESTIONS BASED SOLELY ON THE INFORMATION GIVEN AND NOT ON YOUR OWN OPINIONS OR VIEWS.

VERBAL REASONING QUESTION NUMBER 1

A fire has occurred in a nightclub belonging to Harry James. One person died in the fire, which occurred at 11pm on Saturday night. The club was insured for less than its value.

QUESTIONS – TRUE, FALSE OR IMPOSSIBLE TO SAY?

1. The fire occurred at 1100 hours.

2. A relative of Harry James was killed in the fire.

3. If the insurance company decide to pay out for the fire, Harry James stands to make a profit.

4. The fire was caused by arson.

5. The club was not insured at the time of the fire.

VERBAL REASONING QUESTION NUMBER 2

An accident occurred on the M6 motorway between junctions 8 and 9 southbound at 3pm. The driver of a Ford Fiesta was seen to pull into the middle lane without indicating, forcing another car to veer into the central reservation. One person suffered a broken arm and was taken to hospital before the police arrived.

QUESTIONS – TRUE, FALSE OR IMPOSSIBLE TO SAY?

1. The accident was on the M6 motorway on the carriageway that leads to Scotland.

2. The driver of the Ford Fiesta was injured in the crash.

3. The central reservation was responsible for the accident.

4. The police did not give first aid at the scene.

5. The accident happened at 1500 hours.

VERBAL REASONING QUESTION NUMBER 3

A man of between 30 and 35 years of age was seen stealing a car from outside Mrs Brown's house yesterday. He was seen breaking the nearside rear window with a hammer before driving off at 40 miles per hour. He narrowly missed a young mother who was pushing a pram.

QUESTIONS – TRUE, FALSE OR IMPOSSIBLE TO SAY?

1. The man who stole the car was 34 years old.

2. He stole Mrs Brown's car.

3. The young mother who was pushing a pram was injured.

4. He used a hammer to smash the windscreen.

5. When he drove off he was breaking the speed limit.

VERBAL REASONING QUESTION NUMBER 4

A shopkeeper called Mr Smith was seen serving alcohol to a girl aged 16.

The girl had shown him fake ID, which was a driving licence belonging to her sister. The incident occurred at around 11.30pm on a Wednesday evening during December.

QUESTIONS – TRUE, FALSE OR IMPOSSIBLE TO SAY?

1. The girl is old enough to purchase alcohol from Mr Smith.

2. The girl purchased the alcohol for her sister.

3. The girl's sister had given the driving licence to her.

4. Mr Smith will receive a custodial sentence for his actions.

VERBAL REASONING QUESTION NUMBER 5

Following a bank robbery in a town centre, 6 masked gunmen were seen speeding away from the scene in a black van. The incident, which happened in broad daylight in front of hundreds of shoppers, was picked up by CCTV footage. Police are appealing for witnesses. The local newspaper has offered a £5,000 reward for any information leading to the conviction of all the people involved.

QUESTIONS – TRUE, FALSE OR IMPOSSIBLE TO SAY?

1. The car in which the gunmen drove off was a black van.

2. Someone must have seen something.

3. The incident was picked up by CCTV cameras.

4. The newspaper will pay £5,000 for information leading to the arrest of all of the men involved.

5. Police are not appealing to members of the public for help.

VERBAL REASONING QUESTION NUMBER 6

A factory fire at 'Stevenage Supplies' was arson, the police have confirmed. A man was seen running away from the scene shortly before the fire started. Earlier that day a man was sacked from the company for allegedly stealing money from the safe. The incident is the second one to occur at the factory in as many months.

QUESTIONS – TRUE, FALSE OR IMPOSSIBLE TO SAY?

1. Police have confirmed that the fire at the factory was arson.

2. The man who was seen running away from the fire was the man who started it.

3. One previous 'fire-related' incident has already occurred at the factory.

4. The man who was sacked from the factory may have started the fire.

VERBAL REASONING QUESTION NUMBER 7

At 1800 hours today police issued a statement in relation to the crime scene in Armstrong Road. Police have been examining the scene all day and reports suggest that it may be murder. Forensic officers have been visiting the incident and inform us that the whole street has been cordoned off and nobody will be allowed through. Police say that the street involved will be closed for another 18 hours and no access will be available to anyone during this time.

QUESTIONS – TRUE, FALSE OR IMPOSSIBLE TO SAY?

1. Police have confirmed the incident is murder.

2. Forensic officers have now left the scene.

3. The road will be open at 12 noon the following day.

4. Although the street has been cordoned off, taxis and buses will be given access.

5. Forensic officers will be at the scene all night.

VERBAL REASONING QUESTION NUMBER 8

Mrs Rogers telephoned the police at 8pm to report a burglary at her house in Gamble Crescent. She reports that she came home from work and her front bedroom window was open but she doesn't remember leaving it open.

She informs the police that her jewellery box is missing and also £40 cash, which was left on the kitchen table. She came home from work at 5pm and left again at 7am in the morning. No other signs of forced entry were visible.

QUESTIONS – TRUE, FALSE OR IMPOSSIBLE TO SAY?

1. The burglar made his/her way in through the bedroom window.

2. The burglar took the jewellery and £40 cash before leaving.

3. Mrs Rogers was away from the house for 10 hours in total.

4. Mrs Rogers may have left the window open herself before leaving for work.

5. There were other visible signs of forced entry.

ANSWERS TO VERBAL REASONING QUESTIONS

Question 1

1.   False
2.   Impossible to say
3.   False
4.   Impossible to say
5.   False

Question 2

1.   False
2.   Impossible to say
3.   False
4.   True
5.   True

Question 3

1.   Impossible to say
2.   Impossible to say
3.   False
4.   False
5.   Impossible to say

Question 4

1.   False
2.   Impossible to say
3.   Impossible to say
4.   Impossible to say

Question 5

1. True
2. Impossible to say
3. True
4. False
5. False

Question 6

1. True
2. Impossible to say
3. True
4. True

Question 7

1. False
2. Impossible to say
3. True
4. False
5. Impossible to say

Question 8

1. Impossible to say
2. Impossible to say
3. False
4. True
5. False

Now that you have had the chance to try out a number of verbal reasoning test questions, hopefully you are beginning to grasp what is required. It is very easy to get caught out when answering these types of questions due to the fact that you have to rely solely on the information provided, something that is integral to role of a police officer.

Now try the next set of sample verbal reasoning questions.

VERBAL REASONING QUESTION NUMBER 9

The local bank was held up at gunpoint on Monday the 18th of September at approximately 4pm. The thieves used a black motorcycle to make their getaway. The following facts are also known about the incident:

- Two shots were fired.

- There were 12 staff members on duty at the time of the raid.

- The alarm was raised by the manager and the police were called.

- The cashier was ordered to hand over a bag of money containing £7,000.

- The thieves have not yet been caught.

- Police are appealing for witnesses.

QUESTIONS – TRUE, FALSE OR IMPOSSIBLE TO SAY?

1. The thieves have been caught.

2. The cashier raised the alarm.

3. The cashier was shot.

4. Two people were injured.

5. The bank was open for business at the time of the incident.

VERBAL REASONING QUESTION NUMBER 10

A father and son were found dead in their two-bedroom flat in Sparsbrook on Sunday evening. They had both been suffocated. The following facts are also known:

- The victims were identified by the police as Mark Webster, 16 years old, and his father, Thomas Webster, 39 years old.

- Thomas was in debt to the sum of £37,000.

- Two men were seen leaving the house at 4pm on Sunday afternoon.

- Two men were seen acting suspiciously in the area on Saturday evening before driving off in a Brown Ford Escort car.

- Thomas had previously contacted the police to express his concerns about his safety following threats from his creditors.

- The house had not been broken into.

QUESTIONS – TRUE, FALSE OR IMPOSSIBLE TO SAY?

1. The people Thomas owed money to could have been responsible for the deaths.
2. The two men seen leaving the house were not responsible for the deaths of Mark Webster and Thomas Webster.
3. The house had been broken into.
4. Neighbours reported two men acting suspiciously in the area on Saturday evening.
5. The people responsible for the deaths drove off in a brown Ford Escort car.

VERBAL REASONING QUESTION NUMBER 11

Firefighters have discovered a large quantity of cannabis during a fire on a farm in the village of Teynsville. Police have cordoned off the area. The following facts are also known about the incident:

- The farm is owned by local farmer Peter Watts.

- The fire was deliberately started.

- Peter Watts has two previous convictions for possession and supply of Class A drugs.

- Peter Watts wife was at home on the night of the fire.

- Peter Watts was visiting friends in the nearby town of Grentshill when the fire started.

- A passer-by reported the fire to the police at 9pm.

- Peter Watts has been arrested on suspicion of possession of cannabis.

QUESTIONS – TRUE, FALSE OR IMPOSSIBLE TO SAY?

1. Cannabis is a Class A drug.

2. The fire was started accidentally.

3. A passer-by reported the fire to the fire service at 9pm.

4. The cannabis found during the fire belonged to Peter Watts.

5. Peter Watts has been arrested for possession of cannabis.

VERBAL REASONING QUESTION NUMBER 12

A row of terraced houses was partially destroyed by an explosion on the 17th of April 2007. Just before the explosion a man was seen running back into his house. He had reported a gas leak to the gas board 7 days prior to the explosion. The following facts are also known about the incident:

- The smell of gas had also been reported by two further residents in the weeks leading up to the explosion.

- The police are investigating possible terrorist connections with one of the residents.

QUESTIONS – TRUE, FALSE OR IMPOSSIBLE TO SAY?

1. A gas leak was reported to the gas board on the 10th of April 2007.

2. The explosion was caused by a gas leak.

3. The explosion was not caused by a terrorist attack.

4. The man seen running back into his house had already reported a gas leak to the gas board.

5. The row of terraced houses that were involved in the explosion has been damaged.

ANSWERS TO VERBAL REASONING QUESTIONS

Question number 9

1. False.
2. False.
3. Impossible to say.
4. Impossible to say.
5. Impossible to say.

Question number 10

1. True.
2. Impossible to say.
3. False.
4. Impossible to say.
5. Impossible to say.

Question number 11

1. Impossible to say.
2. False.
3. False.
4. Impossible to say.
5. False.

Question number 12

1. True.
2. Impossible to say.
3. Impossible to say.
4. True.
5. True.

Select the correct statement answer to each of the following verbal reasoning questions.

VERBAL REASONING QUESTION NUMBER 13

At 09.30 this morning Constable Aziz collected the CCTV footage from the Eight to Late Shop on Main Street. He started to review the CCTV footage of the robbery at 14.30 that afternoon. While watching the footage he observed two men, wearing hooded tops (one grey and one green), enter the shop through the door at the back. The time recorded on the footage was 22.45. The men stood at the back of the shop, with only their backs in the view of the CCTV camera. There were four other people in the shop, three customers and a female sales assistant, at the time. The customers were a man and two women.

At 22.47 the two female customers, who appeared to be together, left the shop after paying for three bags of crisps. The other customer paid for a bottle of red wine and left the shop at 22.51. At 22.52 the man in the grey hooded top approached the sales assistant, who was behind the counter at the front of the shop, and appeared to speak to her. At this time the other man was standing near the entrance of the shop. After the exchange with the shop assistant the man took what appeared to be a hand gun from his pocket and waved this in front of the sales assistant. The sales assistant appeared to open the till and then the man seemed to pass a bag over the counter.

At 22.56 the sales assistant started filling the bag. Constable Aziz then observed the shop door open and what appeared to be a man entering the shop. The man who had been standing at the back of the shop stepped forward and punched the man who had been entering the shop. The man who had thrown the punch then shouted at his friend, who then grabbed the bag from the sales assistant and both ran from the shop.

A. The shop was robbed by two men in hoodies in the early hours of the morning.

B. Two men in hoodies were seen by all three people in the shop.

C. CCTV footage shows two men in hoodies committing robbery in the shop with four witnesses.

D. Only the female assistant saw the two men in hoodies.

VERBAL REASONING QUESTION NUMBER 14

A call to Kent police station was made in regards to a hostage in a bank on the local high street. The Bank of HSBC was supposedly being held hostage by 2 men and a woman. It was approximately 16.30 when the police received the call.

As the police got in position outside the bank, they took their time inspecting and regulating the protocol of the upcoming action.

It was said that there was 12 staff on duty and over 10 customers inside the building the moment the building was took hostage.

At 17.05, what appeared to be a gun shot went off. Screams from inside the building echoed onto the streets. The police took a call from the woman who was holding them hostage. "If anyone comes anywhere near the building we start shooting".

The police played a strategic plan in order to prevent anything from happening. But they were running out of options and they were running out of time. The street was becoming darker, with the sudden rainfall falling heavily.

The incident finally come to an end when the police invaded the building, and took the chance of nothing would happen to the hostages.

Everyone was accounted for outside. A guy had been shot in the leg for resisting being taken hostage, but everyone else was not hurt. The only people not to be accounted for was a customer, and one of the guys who took them hostage in the first place.

After the police searching the building, it became apparent

that the customer and the guy was nowhere to be seen in the building, nor the money that was taken from the cashiers.

A. Everyone escaped the bank without being hurt

B. Everyone escaped the bank

C. A customer and a guy who took them hostage had run off with the money that was taken from the bank.

D. All three people who took them hostage left the bank with the money

VERBAL REASONING QUESTION NUMBER 15

At 2130 hours it was dark. The street lights lit up the small neighbourhood of Privet Drive. The fog made it difficult to see clearly. PC Walker was walking down the street of the neighbourhood after he received a call that someone had been broken into. On his arrival, he noticed a distant shadow about 100 yards away from him, as he came closer, the shadow was a person, a teenage boy. The police officer stood quietly talking to the boy, general conversation that was all. The teenage boy had sandy blonde hair, blue eyes, and had a distinctive mole on his left cheek. He was wearing a smart pair of trousers and a polo shirt, and told the officer he was just on his way home from work.

The police officer left the boy and entered No.17, the house that had been broken into. He met the owner of the house in the living room, laying out a plate of biscuits and pouring a cup of tea. Mr David Brown was the owner of house for over 30 years, and claimed that he had never known anything like this to happen in this village.

PC Walker took a look around the house to gather up evidence. He decided to start the investigation upstairs, and as he got to the top of the stairs, he noticed the house had been turned inside out. As if someone had been looking for something. PC Walker asked the owner if he had any pride possessions or anything valuable that could of lead someone to break in and take it. David Brown, looked to floor and quietly whispered, "I had a gun, I've never used it. It was always a safety precaution ever since my late wife Camilla passed away".

PC Walker radioed the station to send out more patrol cars. When asked if he knew anyone that would have taken the gun, David said "no!" Meanwhile, as a few minutes passed, PC Walker came to an assumption. What if the boy he met early on in the night had something to do with it?

Back at the station, other police officers looked at the CCTV of the neighbourhood of Privet Drive. It did not show anything for a good hour or so, and then, in the corner of the screen, they noticed something. A shadow, about 100 yards away from the scene of the crime. The police analysed this further and zoomed in to the shadow, which resembled a person.

A. The teenage boy with sandy blonde hair was caught breaking into David Brown's house

B. CCTV caught the teenage boy breaking into the house

C. PC Walker witnessed the boy breaking into the house

D. CCTV caught the boy about 100 yards away from where the incident took place

VERBAL REASONING QUESTION NUMBER 16

PC Robert Harris was looking through CCTV in regards to a murder of a young local girl from Southampton. The local girl, Mia Tyler was found in a secluded wooded area just off a footpath near her home.

The last moments of Mia on CCTV is 90 minutes before her body was found. At 2130 hours, Mia was caught on CCTV in her local shops about 10 minutes from her house. The police have a 90 minute time gap from the last time she was seen on CCTV until the moments of her death.

Two weeks into the investigation, the Police finally have a lead. A young girl, aged 16 was also in the woods that night walking her dog with her mum and dad. She came across a bag, an identical one to the one Mia was supposedly missing when her body was found. The young girl stated that she did not see or hear anything strange, nothing out of the ordinary.

The police took the bag for forensic DNA testing in hope to find some answers. A breakthrough happened into the investigation, when the Police found fingerprints on the bag of Mia. These fingerprints were not hers, nor were they her families. In fact, the fingerprint belonged to the man who owned the local shop.

Her family said they had known the shop owner for a very long time and would be the last person to hurt their beloved Mia.

A. CCTV caught Mia at the local shops an hour before her body was found

B. The missing bag a young girl finds and the fingerprints the police trace lead them to the local shop owner.

C. Mia's body was found by the local shop owner

D. The fingerprints on the bag was from one of her family members

VERBAL REASONING QUESTION NUMBER 17

At 1630 hours, Constable Robert Nixon interviewed a young boy who was arrested last night. At approximately 2100 hours the night before, a woman, whose name remains anonymous calls the police to tell them that she just witnessed two young boys coming out of a club in Maidstone, and got into a black Vauxhall corsa and drove off. She described the two young boys as being 18-19, and highly intoxicated.

The police sent out two patrol cars to the area in which the woman described. However, the woman did not take note of the number plate, nor did she know what they really looked like. The only useful information she gave was that they were 18-19, both had dark hair and both quite tall.

20 minutes later from the incident being reported, another call was made in regards to a black Vauxhall corsa and that they had crashed into a tree on a country lane just on the outskirts of Maidstone Town Centre. The man who witness the crash, Tom Miles, gave a detailed description of the two young boys, and the police had no doubt that they were the same two boys as the anonymous woman had tried describing earlier.

A. Two people witnessed the young boys crash on the outskirts of Maidstone

B. CCTV showed two boys crash into a tree in Maidstone

C. The police received two phone calls regarding two young boys who seemed to be speaking about the same people.

D. The anonymous female witnessed the young boys crash into the tree

ANSWERS TO VERBAL REASONING

Question number 13

D

Question number 14

C

Question number 15

D

Question number 16

B

Question number 17

C

TIPS FOR PASSING THE VERBAL REASONING TEST

- In the build-up to the assessment, make sure you practice plenty of sample test questions. Little and often is far more effective than cramming the night before your assessment.

- Read the questions carefully. During the test you may have to answer questions that are answered either TRUE, FALSE, or IMPOSSIBLE TO SAY. Base your answers on the evidence supplied only and not on your own views or opinions.

- Do not spend too long on one particular question. If you cannot answer it then move on to the next question but make sure you leave a space on the answer sheet.

- Consider purchasing additional verbal reasoning test booklets or practice aids. You can obtain these through the website www.how2become.com.

- Get plenty of sleep the night before the test. This will allow you to concentrate fully.

NUMERICAL TESTS

As part of the written tests you may also have to sit a numeracy assessment.

The most effective way to prepare for this type of test is to practice sample numerical reasoning tests.

Apart from these sample questions, there are a number of alternative methods for improving your scores. You may wish to invest in a psychometric numerical reasoning test booklet so that you can practice more tests. You can obtain more sample tests through the website www.how2become.com. The more you practice the better you will become at answering these types of questions.

Remember – practice makes perfect!

In the next section I have provided you with a number of sample numeracy tests to help you prepare. Try to answer the questions quickly and without the use of a calculator. You have 5 minutes in which to answer the 14 questions.

NUMERICAL REASONING QUESTIONS – EXERCISE 1

1. A wallet has been found containing one £20 note, five £5 notes, a fifty pence coin and three 2 pence coins. How much is in the wallet?

    Answer

2. Subtract 200 from 500, add 80, subtract 30 and multiply by 2. What number do you have?

    Answer

3. A multi-storey car park has 8 floors and can hold 72 cars on each floor. In addition to this there is also allocation for 4 disabled parking spaces per floor. How many spaces are there in the entire car park?

    Answer

4. A man saves £12.50 per month. How much would he have saved after 1 year?

    Answer

5. If there have been 60 accidents along one stretch of a motorway in the last year, how many on average have occurred each month?

    Answer

6. Out of 40,000 applicants only 4,000 are likely to be successful. What percentage will fail?

Answer [   ]

7. What percentage of 400 is 100?

Answer [   ]

8. Malcolm's shift commences at 0615 hours. If his shift is 10.5 hours long what time will he finish?

Answer [   ]

9. If Mary can bake 12 cakes in 2 hours how many will she bake in 10 hours?

Answer [   ]

10. If there are 24 hours in the day. How many hours are there in one week?

Answer [   ]

11. Susan has 10 coins and gives 5 of them to Steven and the remainder to Alan. Alan gives 3 of his coins to Steven who in turn gives half of his back to Susan. How many is Susan left with?

Answer [   ]

12. Add 121 to 54. Now subtract 75 and multiply by 10. What is the result?

    Answer [   ]

13. Ahmed leaves for work at 8am and arrives at work at 9.17am. He then leaves work at 4.57pm and arrives back at home at 6.03pm. How many minutes has Ahmed spent travelling?

    Answer [   ]

14. A car travels at 30 km/h for the first hour, 65km/h for the second hour, 44 km/h for the third hour and 50 km/h for the fourth hour. What is the car's average speed over the 4-hour journey?

    Answer [   ]

ANSWERS TO NUMERICAL REASONING QUESTIONS – EXERCISE 1

1. £45.56

2. 700

3. 608

4. £150

5. 5

6. 90%

7. 25%

8. 1645 hours or 4.45pm

9. 60 cakes

10. 168

11. 4

12. 1000

13. 143 minutes

14. 47.25 km/h

Now that you have had chance to work through exercise one, try answering the questions that are contained in exercise two. Don't forget to work quickly yet accurately.

NUMERICAL REASONING QUESTIONS – EXERCISE 2

You are not permitted to use a calculator during this exercise.

There are 20 multiple-choice questions and you have 10 minutes in which to answer them all.

1. Your friends tell you their electricity bill has gone up from £40 per month to £47 per month. How much extra are they now paying per year?

   A. £84   **B.** £85   **C.** £83   **D.** £86   **E.** £82

   Answer [   ]

2. A woman earns a salary of £32,000 per year. How much would she earn in 15 years?

   A. £280,000   **B.** £380,000   **C.** £480,000
   D. £260,000   **E.** £460,000

   Answer [   ]

3. If a police officer walks the beat for 6 hours at a pace of 4km/h, how much ground will she have covered after the 6 hours is over?

   A. 20km   **B.** 21km   **C.** 22km   **D.** 23km   **E.** 24km

   Answer [   ]

4. It takes Malcolm 45 minutes to walk 6 miles to work. At what pace does he walk?

A. 7 mph   **B.** 4 mph   **C.** 6 mph   **D.** 5 mph   **E.** 8 mph

Answer

5. Ellie spends 3 hours on the phone talking to her friend abroad. If the call costs 12 pence per 5 minutes, how much does the call cost in total?

A. £3.30   **B.** £4.32   **C.** £3.32   **D.** £4.44   **E.** £3.44

Answer

6. A woman spends £27 in a retail store. She has a discount voucher that reduces the total cost to £21.60. How much discount does the voucher give her?

A. 5%   **B.** 10%   **C.** 15%   **D.** 20%   **E.** 25%

Answer

7. A group of 7 men spend £21.70 on a round of drinks. How much does each of them pay if the bill is split evenly?

A. £3.00   **B.** £65.10   **C.** £3.10   **D.** £3.15   **E.** £3.20

Answer

8. 45,600 people attend a football match to watch Manchester United play Tottenham Hotspur. If there are 32,705 Manchester United supporters at the game, how many Tottenham Hotspur supporters are there?

A. 12,985 **B.** 13,985 **C.** 12, 895
D. 12,895 **E.** 14, 985

Answer

9. The police are called to attend a motorway accident involving a coach full of passengers. A total of 54 people are on board, 17 of whom are injured. How many are not injured?

A. 40 **B.** 39 **C.** 38 **D.** 37 **E.** 36

Answer

10. A car journey usually takes 6 hrs and 55 minutes, but on one occasion the car stops for a total of 47 minutes. How long does the journey take on this occasion?

A. 6 hrs 40 mins **B.** 5 hrs 45 mins **C.** 7 hrs 40 mins
D. 7 hrs 42 mins **E.** 6 hrs 42 mins

Answer

11. There are 10 people in a team. Five of them weigh 70 kg each and the remaining 5 weigh 75 kg each. What is the average weight of the team?

   A. 72.5 kg   **B.** 71.5 kg   **C.** 70.5 kg
   D. 72 kg   **E.** 71 kg

   Answer [   ]

12. A kitchen floor takes 80 tiles to cover. A man buys 10 boxes, each containing 6 tiles. How many more boxes does he need to complete the job?

   A. 2 boxes   **B.** 4 boxes   **C.** 6 boxes
   D. 8 boxes   **E.** 10 boxes

   Answer [   ]

13. How much money does it cost to buy 12 packets of crisps at 47 pence each?

   A. £6.45   **B.** £5.64   **C.** £6.54   **D.** £4.65   **E.** £5.46

   Answer [   ]

14. A motorcyclist is travelling at 78 mph on a road where the speed limit is 50 mph. How much over the speed limit is he?

   A. 20 mph   **B.** 22 mph   **C.** 26 mph
   D. 28 mph   **E.** 30 mph

   Answer [   ]

15. A removal firm loads 34 boxes onto a van. If there are

27 boxes still to be loaded, how many boxes are there in total?

A. 49   **B.** 50   **C.** 61   **D.** 52   **E.** 53

Answer [   ]

16. When paying a bill at the bank you give the cashier one £20 note, two £5 notes, four £1 coins, six 10p coins and two 2p coins. How much have you given him?

A. £34.64   **B.** £43.46   **C.** £34.46
D. £63.44   **E.** £36.46

Answer [   ]

17. If you pay £97.70 per month on your council tax bill, how much would you pay quarterly?

A. £293.30   **B.** £293.20   **C.** £293.10
D. £293.00   **E.** £292.90

Answer [   ]

18. Four people eat a meal at a restaurant. The total bill comes to £44.80. How much do they need to pay each?

A. £10.00   **B.** £10.10   **C.** £10.20
D. £11.10   **E.** £11.20

Answer [   ]

19. A worker is required to work for 8 hours a day. He is

entitled to three 20-minute breaks and one 1-hour lunch break during that 8-hour period. If he works for 5 days per week, how many hours will he have worked after 4 weeks?

A. 12 hours   **B.** 14 hours   **C.** 120 hours
D. 140 hours   **E.** 150 hours

Answer

20. If there are 610 metres in a mile, how many metres are there in 4 miles?

A. 240   **B.** 2040   **C.** 2044   **D.** 2440   **E.** 244

Answer

ANSWERS TO NUMERICAL REASONING QUESTIONS – EXERCISE 2

1. A. £84

In this question you need to first work out the difference in their electricity bill. Subtract £40 from £47 to be left with £7. Now you need to calculate how much extra they are paying per year. If there are 12 months in a year then you need to multiply £7 by 12 months to reach your answer of £84.

2. C. £480,000

The lady earns £32,000 per year. To work out how much she earns in 15 years, you must multiply £32,000 by 15 years to reach your answer of £480,000.

3. E. 24km

To work this answer out all you need to do is multiply the 6 hours by the 4 km/h to reach the total of 24 km. Remember that she is walking at a pace of 4 km per hour for a total of 6 hours.

4. E. 8mph

Malcolm walks 6 miles in 45 minutes, which means he is walking two miles every 15 minutes. Therefore, he would walk 8 miles in 60 minutes (1 hour), so he is walking at 8 mph.

5. B. £4.32

If the call costs 12 pence for every 5 minutes then all you need to do is calculate how many 5 minutes there are in the 3-hour telephone call. There are 60 minutes in every hour, so therefore there are 180 minutes in 3 hours. 180 minutes divided by 5 minutes will give you 36. To get your answer, just multiply 36 by 12 pence to reach your answer of £4.32

6. D. 20%

This type of question can be tricky, especially when you don't have a calculator! The best way to work out the answer is to first of all work out how much 10% discount would give you off the total price. If £27 is the total price, then 10% would be a £2.70 discount. In monetary terms the woman has received £5.40 in discount. If 10% is a £2.70 discount then 20% is a £5.40 discount.

7. C. £3.10

Divide £21.70 by 7 to reach your answer of £3.10.

8. D. 12,895

Subtract 32,705 from 45,600 to reach your answer of 12,895.

9. D. 37

Subtract 17 from 54 to reach your answer of 37.

10. D. 7 hrs 42 minutes

Add the 47 minutes to the normal journey time of 6 hrs and 55 minutes to reach your answer of 7 hrs and 42 minutes.

11. A. 72.5 kg

To calculate the average weight, you need to first of all add each weight together. Therefore, $(5 \times 70) + (5 \times 75) = 725$ kg. To find the average weight you must now divide the 725 by 10, which will give you the answer 72.5 kg.

12. B. 4 boxes

The man has 10 boxes, each of which contains 6 tiles. He therefore has a total of 60 tiles. He now needs a further 20 tiles to cover the total floor area. If there are 6 tiles in a box then he will need a further 4 boxes (24 tiles).

13. B. £5.64

Multiply 12 by 47 pence to reach your answer of £5.64.

14. D. 28 mph

Subtract 50 mph from 78 mph to reach your answer of 28 mph.

15. C. 61

Add 34 to 27 to reach your answer of 61 boxes.

16. A. £34.64

Add all of the currency together to reach the answer of £34.64.

17. C. £293.10

To reach the answer you must multiply £97.70 by 3. Remember, a quarter is every 3 months.

18. E. £11.20

Divide £44.80 by 4 people to reach your answer of £11.20.

19. C. 120 hours

First of all you need to determine how many 'real' hours he works each day. Subtract the total sum of breaks from 8 hours to reach 6 hours per day. If he works 5 days per week then he is working a total of 30 hours per week. Multiply 30 hours by 4 weeks to reach your answer of 120 hours.

20. D. 2440 metres

Multiply 4 by 610 metres to reach your answer of 2440 metres.

TIPS FOR PASSING THE NUMERICAL REASONING TEST

- Try plenty of sample test questions in the build-up to the assessment.

- Use a calculator when carrying out the test questions. You are permitted to use a calculator during the real test so it is important that you become competent in the use of one. The calculator will be supplied by the assessment centre.

- Try to work quickly yet accurately through the test. If you miss a question then make sure you leave a gap on the answer sheet.

- If you generally struggle with this type of test then consider getting a personal tutor.

- During the test do not concentrate on the other candidates and how fast they are working. Keep your head down and focus only on your own performance.

In order to further assist you during your preparation I will now provide you with a further sample numerical ability test. Once again, the questions that follow will not be the ones you will get asked during the actual numerical ability test; however, they will go a long way to helping you to prepare fully for the assessment centre.

PRACTICE TEST 3

1. If 70% of £500 has been spent, how much money remains?

   A. £125   **B.** £130   **C.** £140   **D.** £150   **E.** £160

   Answer _____

2. A multi-storey office has 7 floors, and each floor has 49 employees. How many members of staff work in the multi-storey office?

   A. 257   **B.** 343   **C.** 357   **D.** 423   **E.** 475

   Answer _____

3. Following some road works on the M1 the Highways Agency need their 5 vehicles to collect 1,250 cones. If each vehicle collects the same amount of cones, how many cones does each individual vehicle collect?

   A. 125   **B.** 200   **C.** 250   **D.** 500   **E.** 525

   Answer _____

4. Laura buys three items: a pair of shoes, a dress, and a coat. The items totalled £340. If the shoes were £59.99 and the coat was £139.99, how much was the dress?

   A. £138.02   **B.** £138.00   **C.** £140.02   **D.** £142.00   **E.** £144.00

   Answer _____

5. At Telford school there are 200 school students. 25
    students get straight A's. What is this as a percentage?

    A. 12.5%   **B.** 10%   **C.** 15%   **D.** 30%   **E.** 25%

    Answer [   ]

6. A carton of milk costs £1.19. How much change would
    you have left from £5.00 if you bought one carton?

    A. £2.81   **B.** £3.61   **C.** £3.71   **D.** £3.81   **E.** £4.05

    Answer [   ]

7. You are driving down a motorway at 108 mph. How far
    do you travel in 25 minutes?

    A. 47 miles   **B.** 45 miles   **C.** 44 miles
    D. 42 miles   **E.** 41 miles

    Answer [   ]

8. A fast jet is flying at a speed of 270 mph. The distance
    from airfield A to airfield B is 90 miles. How long does it
    take to fly from A to B?

    A. 20 minutes   **B.** 24 minutes   **C.** 22 minutes
    D. 26 minutes   **E.** 28 minutes

    Answer [   ]

9. You are travelling down a motorway. Your journey has lasted 50 minutes and you have covered 125 miles. What speed have you been travelling at?

   A. 162 mph   **B.** 155 mph   **C.** 160 mph
   D. 152 mph   **E.** 150 mph

   Answer

10. The AA on average responds to 25 calls a day. How many do they respond to in a week?

    A. 160   **B.** 165   **C.** 170   **D.** 175   **E.** 180

    Answer

11. Lincolnshire, Yorkshire and Lancashire all have new police helicopters. It takes the Lincolnshire helicopter 15 minutes to fly to Leeds, the Lancashire helicopter takes 35 minutes and the Yorkshire helicopter takes 10 minutes. What is the average time it takes these three helicopters to get to Leeds?

    A. 15 minutes   **B.** 20 minutes   **C.** 25 minutes
    D. 30 minutes   **E.** 35 minutes

    Answer

12. A car park has 500 available spaces. On a busy day 75% of these are full. How many full car parking spaces are there on a busy day?

    A. 375   **B.** 350   **C.** 325   **D.** 320   **E.** 310

    Answer

13. You have £50 in your wallet and spend 70% of it on shopping. How much money have you spent on shopping?

   A. £30   **B.** £35   **C.** £40   **D.** £50   **E.** £45

   Answer [   ]

14. The RSPCA has 120,000 officers. 3% of these officers are due to retire. How many officers will retire?

   A. 360,000   **B.** 36,000   **C.** 360   **D.** 36   **E.** 3,600

   Answer [   ]

15. The road tax for your car cost £120 in 2007. In 2008 it inoroaooo by 10%. How much is the road tax in 2008?

   A. £121.20   **B.** £132   **C.** £142   **D.** £152   **E.** £152.20

   Answer [   ]

16. A school decides to buy 12 laptops costing £850 each. What is the combined cost for the 12 laptops?

   A. £10,200   **B.** £10,400   **C.** £10,500
   D. £10,600   **E.** £10,800

   Answer [   ]

17. A metre of wool costs 62p. How much would it cost to buy 6 metres of wool?

   A. £3.72   **B.** £3.62   **C.** £3.82   **D.** £4.72   **E.** £5.12

   Answer [   ]

18. Sally is riding her horse in a cross country competition. She has been told that she has to complete the course in 2 hours and 30 minutes. If divided into equal quarters, how long should she aim to spend completing each phase?

A. 35 minutes   **B.** 37.5 minutes   **C.** 35.5 minutes
       D. 38.5 minutes   **E.** 39.5 minutes

Answer

19. There are 18 teams entered in a rugby competition. If there are 6 changing rooms, how many teams use each changing room?

A. 2   **B.** 4   **C.** 6   **D.** 3   **E.** 5

Answer

20. Using the diagram below, calculate the perimeter of the inner rectangle?

A. 16.4 cm

B. 17.2 cm

C. 17.8 cm

D. 18.4 cm

E. 18.8 cm

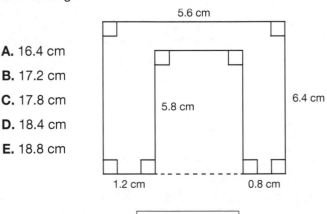

Answer

21. A room measures 20m by 5m. If I wanted to carpet 50% of it and I had 60 square metres of carpet available, how many square metres would I have left after finishing the task?

    A. 5m²   **B.** 10m²   **C.** 15m²   **D.** 20m²   **E.** 25m²

    Answer [   ]

22. If a ferry journey of 490 miles takes 7 hours, what is the average speed of the ferry?

    A. 55 mph   **B.** 60 mph   **C.** 65 mph
    D. 70 mph   **E.** 80 mph

    Answer [   ]

23. A multi-storey car park has 8 levels. Each level has 111 car parking spaces. How many cars will be in the car park when it is full?

    A. 784   **B.** 888   **C.** 988   **D.** 8,888   **E.** 9,988

    Answer [   ]

24. The office sweepstake wins £1,500. If this is divided by 25 employees, how much does each employee win?

    A. £30   **B.** £40   **C.** £60   **D.** £80   **E.** £85

    Answer [   ]

ANSWERS TO PRACTICE TEST 3

Answer to question 1

The word 'of' means multiply in mathematics.

Therefore 70% of £500 = 70% × £500

To calculate this, first convert 70% into a decimal. Any percentage can be converted into a decimal by dividing it by 100.

70% = 70 ÷ 100 = 0.7

70% × £500 = 0.7 × £500 = £350

This means that £350 has been spent. The remaining money, out of £500 can be found by subtracting the money spent (£350) from £500.

Money remaining = £500 − £350 = £150

The answer to question 1 is **D. £150**

Answer to question 2

If there are 7 floors and on each floor there are 49 employees, then in total there must by:

Total number of staff in the multi-storey office = 49 × 7 = 343

The answer to question 2 is **B. 343**

Answer to question 3

There are 1,250 cones and only 5 vehicles to collect them all. If each vehicle collects the same amount of cones then this means that the number of cones are split equally between all 5 vehicles. Therefore to calculate how many cones each individual vehicle collects simply divide the total amount of cones by the number of vehicles:

Amount of cones each vehicle collects = 1,250 ÷ 5 = 250 *cones*

The answer to question 3 is **C. 250**

Answer to question 4

If all 3 items totalled £340, then simply subtract the price of the two items that you already know to leave the price of a dress, which equals £140.02 as shown below.

The total cost of buying all three items is £340. This can be written in an equation form as shown below.

Price of Pair of shoes + Price of Dress + Price of Coat = £340

To find how much the dress was, the equation can be rearranged so that:

Price of Dress = £340 – *Price of Pair of shoes* – *Price of Coat*

Now the price of shoes and the price of a coat can be put into the above equation:

Price of Dress = £340 – £59.99 – £139.99 = £140.02

The answer to question 4 is **C. £140.02**

Answer to question 5

Out of 200 school students, 25 of them get A's. As a fraction this can be written as:

$$\frac{25}{200}$$

It is important to now recall that percentages are always out of 100. The fraction above is currently out of 200. If the lower half of the fraction is divided by 2, then the fraction will be out of 100 as shown below:

$$\frac{25}{200} = \frac{12.5}{100} \qquad \div 2$$

To convert a fraction that is out of 100 into a percentage simply multiply it by 100 as shown below:

$$\frac{12.5}{100} \times 100\% = 12.5\%$$

Note that the 100 from the lower half (denominator) of the fraction cancels with the 100 that is used to multiply the fraction with to leave 12.5%

The answer to question 5 is **A. 12.5%**

Answer to question 6

There are two methods of calculating change. One is to count up and the other is to count down.

Method 1 (The count up method)

The carton of milk costs £1.19. You have £5. To work out how much change I would get I count up from £1.19 until I get to £5.

So, £1.19 add another £3 would give:

£1.19 + £3 = £4.19

This does not yet add up to £5 in total, so I know that I am due more change than £3. I can get from £4.19 to £5 by adding 81p. In total, I have needed to add £3.81 to £1.19 in order to make £5.

This means that the change I should get from £5 if a carton of milk costs £1.19 is £3.81

Method 2 (The countdown method)

The change can also be calculated by simply subtracting the cost of the product from the amount of money used to pay for it. So if I were to give £5 to the cashier when paying for a product that cost £1.19, the change would be calculated as shown below:

Change = £5 − £1.19 = £3.81

The answer to question 6 is **D. £3.81**

Answer to question 7

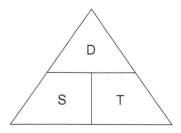

In the above triangle:

D represents Distance
S represents Speed
T represents Time.

If you wanted a formula to calculate distance D, simply place your thumb over D on the triangle. You will now see that D = S × T

The formula to use here is:

Distance (in miles) = speed (mph) × time (hours)

The first thing that needs to be done is to convert 25 minutes into hours. This can be achieved by dividing 25 by 60:

25 minutes in hour = $\dfrac{25}{60}$ = 0.416666 *hours*

It is now possible to use the distance formula:

Distance (in miles) = speed (mph) × time (hours)

= 108 *mph* × 0.416666 *hours*

= 45 *miles*

The answer to question 7 is **B. 45 miles**

NOTE: Speed, distance and time questions do not usually form part of the police officer numerical ability test.

Answer to question 8

This question is asking you to calculate a time.

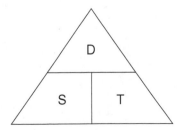

In the above triangle:

D represents Distance
S represents Speed
T represents Time.

If you wanted a formula to calculate time, T, simply place your thumb over T on the triangle. You will now see that $T = D \div S$

The formula to use here is:

Time (in hours) = distance (miles) ÷ speed (miles per hour)

$= 90$ *miles* $\div 270$ *mph*

$= 0.333333$ *hours*

To find what 0.3333 hours is in minutes, multiply 0.33333 hours by 60 as there are 60 minutes in 1 hour.

0.333333 hours × 60 = 20 minutes

The answer to question 8 is **A. 20 minutes**

Answer to question 9

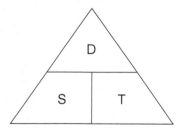

If you wanted a formula to calculate speed, simply place your thumb over S on the triangle. You will now see that $S = D \div T$

The formula to use here is:

$$Speed\ (mph) = \frac{distance\ (miles)}{time\ (hour)}$$

The question gives the distance as 125 miles. Miles are the correct units to use for the formula and therefore 125 miles can be put straight into the formula without converting it to any other unit. The journey time is given as 50 minutes. The time written as 50 minutes cannot be used in the formula for speed shown above. The time in minutes must be converted into hours before it can be used in the above formula. To convert 50 minutes into hours only use the procedure below:

To convert 50 minutes into hours, divide it by 60 minutes as there are 60 minutes in 1 hour:

50 minutes converted into hours = 50 ÷ 60 = 0.83333 *hours*

This can now be used in the formula for speed:

$$Speed\ (mph) = \frac{125\ (miles)}{0.8333\ (hour)}$$

= 150 *mph*

The answer to question 9 is **E. 150 mph**

Answer to question 10

There are 7 days in a week. If the AA responds to 25 calls a day, then to find how many calls they respond to in a week multiply 25 by 7.

Calls responded to in a week = 25 × 7 = 175

The answer to question 10 is **D. 175**

Answer to question 11

An average is calculated by adding together all the individual times it took each helicopter to fly to Leeds and dividing by how many helicopters there are.

Average time = (15 + 35 + 10) ÷ 3

= 60 ÷ 3 = 20 *minutes*

The answer to question 11 is **B. 20 minutes**

Answer to question 12

75% of the 500 available spaces are full on a busy day. The word 'of' in mathematics means multiply. Therefore, to calculate 75% of 500 convert 75% into a decimal and then multiply it by 500. This will give the amount of full car parking spaces on a 'busy' day.

Step 1: Convert 75% into a decimal. To convert a percentage into a decimal, divide the percentage by 100:

75% = 75 ÷ 100 = 0.75

Step 2: Multiply 500 by 0.75 to find how many parking spaces are full on a busy day:

500 × 0.75 = 375

The answer to question 12 is **A. 375 parking spaces** were full on a busy day.

Answer to question 13

This question states that you spent 70% of the £50 in your wallet. The word 'of' in mathematics means multiply and therefore the same method used to solve question 12 can be used here.

Step 1: Convert 70% into a decimal. To convert a percentage into a decimal, divide the percentage by 100:

70% = 70 ÷ 100 = 0.7

Step 2: Multiply £50 by 0.75 to find how much money was spent on shopping:

£50 × 0.7 = £35

The answer to question 13 is **B. £35** was spent on shopping.

Answer to question 14

This question states that 3% of the 120,000 officers in the RSPCA are due to retire. The word 'of' in mathematics means multiply and therefore the same method used to solve questions 12 and 13 can be used here.

Step 1: Convert 3% into a decimal. To convert a percentage into a decimal, divide the percentage by 100:

3% = 3 ÷ 100 = 0.03

Step 2: Multiply 120,000 (the amount of officers in the RSPCA) by 0.03 to find how many officers will retire:

120,000 × 0.03 = 3,600

The answer to question 14 is **E. 3,600 officers** are due to retire from the RSPCA.

Answer to question 15

Any number can be increased by a percentage by converting the percentage into a decimal then adding 1 to that decimal and then multiplying the decimal by the number you want to increase by a percentage.

Step 1: Convert the percentage into a decimal by dividing the percentage by 100.

$10\% = 10 \div 100 = 0.1$

Step 2: Add 1 to the decimal

$1 + 0.1 = 1.1$

Step 3: Now multiply the cost of road tax in 2007 by 1.10 in order to find out what the new cost in 2008 for road tax is.

£120 × 1.1 = 3,600

This means that road tax has increased in value by £12 and now costs £132 in 2008 rather than £120 as it did in 2007.

The answer to question 15 is **B. £132**

Answer to question 16

Method 1

The price of one laptop is £850. If you wanted two of these laptops you would add £850 twice:

Price of 2 laptops = £850 + £850 = £1,700

If you wanted 3 laptops, you would add £850 three times:

Price of 3 laptops = £850 + £850 + £850 = £2,550

If you wanted 4 laptops, you would add £850 four times and

so on. So if you wanted 12 laptops, priced at £850 each, you would need to add £850 twelve times.

Price of 12 laptops = £850 + £850 + £850 + £850 + £850 + £850 + £850 + £850 + £850 + £850 + £850 + £850 = £10,200

12 laptops priced at £850 each would cost £10,200

Method 2

There is a quicker alternative to adding £850 twelve times. Simply multiply £850 by 12 which gives the same result as adding £850 together twelve times.

Price of 12 laptops = £850 × 12 = £10,200

The answer to question 16 is **A. £10,200**

Answer to question 17

One metre of wool costs 62p. Buying 6 of these would equal:

Cost of 6 metres of wool = 62p × 6 = 372p

To convert any amount of pence into pound, divide the pence by 100 because 100 pence makes £1.

372p = 372 ÷ 100 = £3.72

Alternatively, you could add 62p six times to get the answer:

Cost of 6 metres of wool = 62p + 62p + 62p + 62p + 62p + 62p = 372p

And 372p= £3.72

The answer to question 17 is **A. £3.72**

Answer to question 18

Firstly work out how many minutes Sally has to complete the course in. There are 60 minutes in 1 hour. This means that in 2 hours, there are:

$60 \times 2 = 120$ *minutes*

In total Sally has been told that she has 2 hours and 30 minutes to complete the course. 2 hours represents 120 minutes, then simply add on 30 minutes to this:

2 hours 30 minutes = 120 minutes + 30 minutes = 150 minutes

The next part of the question states: *"If divided into equal quarters, how long should she aim to spend completing each phase?"*

A quarter means 'out of 4'. So to work out how long she should aim to spend completing each phase, divide the total minutes (150) by 4:

$150 \div 4 = 37.5$ *minutes*

Sally should aim to complete each phase in 37.5 minutes.

The answer to question 18 is **B. 37.5 minutes**

Answer to question 19

18 teams need to share 6 changing rooms between them. To calculate how many teams use each changing room, divide the total number of teams by the number of changing rooms available to be used.

$18 \div 6 = 3$ *teams in each changing room*

The answer to question 19 is **D. 3**

Answer to question 20

A perimeter of an object is defined as the total length of all sides of the object. For the inner rectangle shown, both the longer sides are known. It's just the length of the dotted line at the bottom of the rectangle that we don't know.

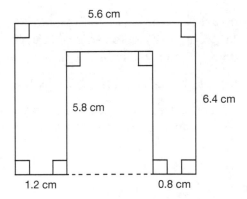

The top line of the outer, larger rectangle is 5.6 cm. This means that the entire bottom line must equal 5.6 cm. Two lengths on the bottom line are already given. To find the missing length, which is the dotted line, call x the length of the dotted line:

$1.2\ cm + 0.8\ cm + x\ cm = 5.6\ cm$

$x\ cm = 5.6 - 1.2 - 0.8 = 3.6\ cm$

The lengths of the inner rectangle are:

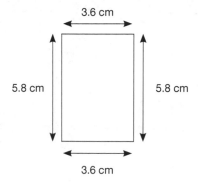

Adding the lengths of all sides of the rectangle will give the perimeter.

Perimeter = 3.6 + 3.6 + 5.8 + 5.8 = 18.8 *cm*

The answer to question 20 is **E. 18.8 cm**

Answer to question 21

Firstly calculate how many square metres the room measures by finding its area. This can be achieved by multiplying the two measurements together.

Area of the room = 20 *m* × 5 *m* = 100 *m²*

50% of anything is half of it, which means that 50% of 100m² would equal 50m². If you are not convinced, the calculation would be to convert 50% into a decimal and then multiply it by 100 m2:

Step 1: Convert 50% into a decimal by dividing it by 100:

50% = 50 ÷ 100 = 0.5

Step 2: Multiply 0.5 by 100m^2

$0.5 \times 100 \ m^2 = 50 \ m^2$

If someone has 60 m^2 of carpet but only needs to use 50m2 of carpet then there would be:

$60 \ m^2 - 50 \ m^2 = 10 \ m^2$ of carpet left over.

The answer to question 21 is **B. 10m^2**

Answer to question 22

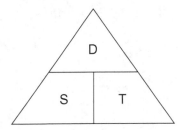

If you wanted a formula to calculate speed, simply place your thumb over S on the triangle. You will now see that $S = D \div T$

The formula to use here is:

$$Speed \ (mph) = \frac{distance \ (miles)}{time \ (hour)}$$

$= 490 \ miles \div 7 \ hours = 70 \ mph$

The answer to question 22 is **D. 70 mph**

Answer to question 23

1 level at the car park contains 111 car parking spaces. This means that 8 levels will contain 8 times this amount.

Cars in the car park when it is full = 8 × 111 *cars* = 888 *cars*

The answer to question 23 is **B. 888 cars**

Answer to question 24

The answer can be found by dividing the total win by how many employees there are. This will split the amount equally between all employees:

£1,500 ÷ 25 = £60

Each employee wins £60.

The answer to question 24 is **C. £60**

PRACTICE TEST 4

QUESTION 1.

Kent Police have put out a tender for heating maintenance and installation. Below are quotes from 3 suppliers.

Heating maintenance and installation	Supplier 1 Total cost over 3 years (£)	Supplier 2 Total cost over 2 years (£)	Supplier 3 Total cost over 5 years (£)
Installation and boiler replacements	24,630	19,750	36,150
Hot Air Systems	142,530	102,640	229,850
Service and maintenance	17,880	12,460	25,625

1. Amongst all three suppliers, based on an annual cost, what is the average cost to install hot air systems?

   A. 45804

   B. 50000

   C. 48266

   D. 47655

2. Based on 2 years, what supplier provides the most expensive quote for installation and boiler replacements?

   A. Supplier 1

   B. Supplier 2

   C. Supplier 3

   D. Suppler 1 and 3

3. What percentage of the total quote provided by Supplier 2 accounts for hot air systems?

    A. 75%

    B. 76.1%

    C. 77.4%

    D. 73.9%

QUESTION 2.

The Police Headquarters have put out a tender for security checks and system updates. Below are quotes from 3 suppliers.

Security checks and system updates	**Supplier 1** Total cost over 2 years (£)	**Supplier 2** Total cost over 4 years (£)	**Supplier 3** Total cost over 5 years (£)
Basic Security Check	26,330	40,560	52,550
Advanced Security Check	52,530	104,320	120,880
Updating software and security	15,430	31,220	32,000

1. What percentage of the total quote provided by Supplier 2 accounts for updating software and security?

    A. 12.4%

    B. 17.7%

    C. 19.2%

    D. None of these

2. For the total cost over 5 years, what supplier provides the cheapest quote overall for security checks and system updates?

   A. Supplier 1
   B. Supplier 2
   C. Supplier 3
   D. Supplier 1 and 2

3. Based on an annual cost, what supplier provides the most expensive quote for basic security cost?

   A. Supplier 1
   B. Supplier 2
   C. Supplier 3
   D. All the same

QUESTION 3.

The Police Headquarters have put out a tender for fitness testing. Below are quotes from 3 suppliers.

Fitness Testing	Supplier 1 Total cost over 2 years (£)	Supplier 2 Total cost over 3 years (£)	Supplier 3 Total cost over 4 years (£)
Basic Fitness Training	9,800	10,500	16,650
Intense Fitness Training	19,000	23,500	34,500
8 week Fitness Programme	16,000	18,000	33,000

1. What percentage of the total quote provided by Supplier 2 accounts for intense fitness training?

   A. 43.5%
   B. 45.2%
   C. 46%
   D. 44.9%

2. Based on an annual one year cost, which supplier provides the most expensive overall quote for basic fitness training?

   A. Supplier 1
   B. Supplier 2
   C. Supplier 3
   D. Supplier 1 and 3

3. Based on an annual one year cost, which supplier provides the cheapest 8 week Fitness programme?

   A. Supplier 1
   B. Supplier 2
   C. Supplier 3
   D. All the same

QUESTION 4.

Kent Police have put out a tender for uniform dry cleaning and alterations. Below are quotes from 3 suppliers.

Uniform dry cleaning and amendments	**Supplier 1** Total cost over 1 years (£)	**Supplier 2** Total cost over 3 years (£)	**Supplier 3** Total cost over 2 years (£)
Dry Cleaning	9,600	26,700	19,020
Alterations	5,500	14,900	11,000
Cleaning and alterations – Full package	13,450	38,850	25,800

1. Based on an annual one year cost, which supplier provides the cheapest dry cleaning services?

   A. Supplier 1

   B. Supplier 2

   C. Supplier 3

   D. All the same

2. For the total cost over 3 years, what supplier provides the cheapest quote overall for cleaning and alterations – full package?

   A. Supplier 1

   B. Supplier 2

   C. Supplier 3

   D. All the same

3. Based on an annual cost and everything the supplier has to offer, what supplier is the most expensive?

   A. Supplier 1
   B. Supplier 2
   C. Supplier 3
   D. All the same

QUESTION 5.

Kent Police have put out a tender for electrical equipment and supplies. Below are quotes from 3 suppliers.

Electrical Equipment and supplies	**Supplier 1** Total cost over 2 years (£)	**Supplier 2** Total cost over 2 years (£)	**Supplier 3** Total cost over 1 years (£)
Basic Services	34,550	36,660	15,450
Electrical safety Check	39,550	42,000	20,000
Full Equipment Maintenance	120,850	150,500	60,000

1. Based on an annual year cost, which supplier offers the best price for electrical safety checks?

   A. Supplier 1
   B. Supplier 2
   C. Supplier 3
   D. They are the same

2. What percentage of the total quote provided by supplier 1 accounts for basic services?

A. 17%

B. 17.7%

C. 18.5%

D. 18.3%

3. Based on 2 years, what supplier provides the cheapest quote overall for electrical equipment and supplies?

A. Supplier 1

B. Supplier 2

C. Supplier 3

D. Supplier 2 and 3

ANSWERS TO PRACTICE TEST 4

Question 1

1. Amongst all three suppliers, based on an annual cost, what is the average cost to install hot air systems?

   Answer - 48266

2. Based on 2 years, what supplier provides the most expensive quote for installation and boiler replacements?

   Answer - Supplier 2

3. What percentage of the total quote provided by Supplier 2 accounts for hot air systems?

   Answer - 76.1

Question 2

1. What percentage of the total quote provided by Supplier 2 accounts for updating software and security?

   Answer - 17.7%

2. For the total cost over 5 years, what supplier provides the cheapest quote overall for security   checks and system updates?

   Answer - Supplier 3

3. Based on an annual cost, what supplier provides the most expensive quote for installation and boiler replacements?

   Answer – Supplier 1

Question 3

1. What percentage of the total quote provided by Supplier 2 accounts for intense fitness training?

    Answer – 45.2

2. Based on an annual one year cost, which supplier provides the most expensive overall quote for basic fitness training?

    Answer – Supplier 1

3. Based on an annual one year cost, which supplier provides the cheapest 8 week Fitness programme?

    Answer – Supplier 2

Question 4

1. Based on an annual one year cost, which supplier provides the cheapest dry cleaning services?

    Answer – Supplier 2

2. For the total cost over 3 years, what supplier provides the cheapest quote overall for cleaning and alterations – full package?

    Answer – Supplier 3

3. Based on an annual cost and everything the supplier has to offer, what supplier is the most expensive?

    Answer – Supplier 1

Question 5

1. Based on an annual year cost, which supplier offers the best price for electrical safety checks?

   Answer - Supplier 1

2. What percentage of the total quote provided by supplier 1 accounts for basic services?

   Answer - 17.7%

3. Based on 2 years, what supplier provides the cheapest quote overall for electrical equipment and supplies?

   Answer - Supplier 3

THE WRITTEN EXERCISES – REPORT WRITING

During the assessment centre you will be asked to take two written exercises. These will require you to create an **Incident Report Form**, based on the information given during the exercise. The following is an overview of the two exercises that you will have to carry out:

Written Exercise One. In this exercise, you will need to deal with a customer. The customer will be writing in to complain about how an incident was dealt with by your centre's security guard. You will be given 7 different sheets of paper, each containing a different take (from different witnesses) on the incident. Normally one of these will be from the security guard, detailing his view. You may or may not also be given CCTV based evidence (in written form) to look over. All 7 witness reports will differ, and therefore there will be discrepancies.

Your job is to write down the facts of the case, and at the end, make a recommendation about what should be done.

Written Exercise Two. In this exercise, you will watch a 12 minute DVD of an interview between a witness to an incident at a shopping centre, and the security staff working at the centre. You will allowed to take notes during the screening, but there will be no pauses or breaks, and therefore you will need to take down as much important information as possible whilst watching the DVD. Your job is to take down all of the facts, and construct this into an incident report form, all whilst watching the DVD.

When you create a written report, the assessor is looking for a well-structured piece of writing that is logical and relevant. You should demonstrate a good use and understanding of grammar, and aim to make zero spelling or grammatical errors. **This is extremely important**. You also need to make sure that your handwriting is neat and tidy, as this could reflect badly with your assessors.

The biggest factor in passing or failing this assessment, is your attention to detail. You cannot afford to miss key pieces of evidence or facts of the case, as you will be penalised for this. A great way to practice for the first exercise in particular is to look at a magazine or newspaper which reports on a particular event. Take a pen and paper, look through the story and then try to write down the key facts about the case.

The written report is an area of the police officer assessment process that many people do not think they need to practice. They use their preparation time before their assessment date predominantly looking at the role-plays and the interview. The written report can actually gain you the highest percentage of marks out of all the assessment tests. This could mean the difference between a pass and a fail.

WHAT IS AN INCIDENT REPORT FORM?

An Incident Report Form refers to a written summary of the facts of the incident. For example, what clothes the suspect was wearing, the consequences of the crime, what was stolen and what time the incident occurred. As I have mentioned, you should aim to take a structured approach to your report, which quickly relays the factual details of the incident and does not give any irrelevant information.

On the following page, I have provided you with an example of what you might expect to see in the two written exercises.

INCIDENT REPORT FORM: EXERCISE 1

Take a look at the following passage, and then construct an incident report form based on what you read.

At 21:17 on the 24th August 2015, a man was seeing running away from Al's Pizza Restaurant, down Ficshire Lane. A witness reported seeing the man leap over a garden fence, disappearing from view. At 21:19, the fire service were called to the restaurant, as the entire left hand side wall of the building had gone up in flames. Unfortunately, this resulted in 3 fatalities, and a further 2 people were taken to hospital with serious injuries. Further investigation has revealed that the fire was a result of arson. The owner of the restaurant has revealed that he is devastated by the impact of the blaze, and has apologised sincerely to the families who have been impacted.

The witness in question was named Norris. He has white hair, glasses and a goatee beard. He works at the local confectionary shop and was just closing up for the night, when he noticed the man running away down the street. Norris described the man as having short blonde hair, with a fringe over his eyes, wearing red tracksuit bottoms and a green sweatshirt. He believes that the man was 5 ft 7 in height and wore glasses. Norris claims that he would have tackled the man himself, but he has a bad hip and has just come out of surgery. Therefore, he could not chase the man.

Norris claims that he shouted after the man, but the individual did not respond. When he went to look over the fence, at house number 94, the man had gone. At the scene, a can of petrol was found, along with a lighter and an old bus receipt. The taxi station next door to the restaurant closed down 2 days ago, after the owner went bankrupt.

HOW TO ANSWER THIS

As I have mentioned, the best way to answer this type of question is to carefully go through the passage, and make sure that you are clear on what is relevant and what is irrelevant. For example, looking at the passage, you should be able to notice that how the witness looks is entirely irrelevant. For this reason, you shouldn't include such information in your report, and you will be penalised for doing so. Think only about what matters to the case. Essentially, all you are being asked to do is summarise the key facts. Providing you are observant, this shouldn't be too difficult.

Now, take a look at our sample Incident Report Form, based on the passage:

Sample Response

The following has been written in response to the incident that occurred at 21:17 on the 24th August 2015, at Ficshire Lane.

The incident in question surrounds a fire that took place at Al's Pizza Restaurant. At 21:19, the fire service were called to tackle a blaze that had engulfed the entire left hand wall of the building. Unfortunately, this incident resulted in 3 deaths, and 2 further people being taken to hospital with serious injuries. An investigation into the incident has revealed that the fire was a result of arson. Therefore, a criminal investigation needs to be launched.

To add to the criminal investigation, we have the testimony of a shop worker who was walking home past the scene of the crime. He claims to have seen a man with short blonde hair and a fringe over his glasses, running away from the scene. The man was wearing red tracksuit bottoms and a green sweatshirt, and was 5 ft 7 in height. When the witness called out to him, he was ignored. The man jumped over a garden fence and then escaped from view. This man is high priority and needs to be questioned immediately by the police.

Evidence found at the scene included a can of petrol, a lighter and an old bus receipt.

Now that you've seen how to tackle this type of question, take a look at the question below, and try to construct your own response based on the passage:

INCIDENT REPORT FORM: EXERCISE 2

On the afternoon of 14th May 2015, police were called to an incident at a house in West Ficshire. They entered the premises at 17:17, to discover a crying child, blood on the floor and a woman locked in a bedroom. The child was the person who had called the police. He claims that his father, John Jacob, assaulted his mother after an argument. John Jacobs is a car engineer who runs his own business in South Ficshire. He has been in charge of the company for 4 years, after previously working in sales administration. The boy claims that his mother locked herself in the bedroom, after a punch to the jaw left her bleeding heavily. The boy's mother is named Mary Jacob, and works at a sewing factory. After unlocking the bedroom door, Mary Jacob corroborated her son's account of events.

The police also decided to interview the Jacobs' next door neighbours. The neighbours are named Mary-Sue Smith and Jonathon Smith. Mary-Sue works at a publishing firm, and Jonathon works as a housing developer. Mary-Sue has short white hair and walks with the aid of a cane. She claims that she heard violent shouting from next door, followed by the sound of a woman begging a man not to hit her. She then heard a bedroom door slam, followed by the front door opening and a car screeching away outside. She told the police that John Jacob drives a red Aston Martin, with the number plate PPY 727Z.

Mr Jacob has not been seen since the incident, and is wanted by the police.

Sample Response

INCIDENT REPORT FORM: EXERCISE 3

As we have mentioned, during the first part of the written exercise, you will be given statements from various witnesses to an incident. The above exercises should have given you a good idea of how to answer this. Now, let's look at an exercise which contains direct statements from witnesses. Read through the below information and then have a go at answering the question.

An incident has occurred at Ficshire shopping centre. One of the customers had written in to complain that a security guard behaved aggressively towards her, and tried to steal her bag. Below are 3 witness statements from the event. Read through them carefully and lay out the facts in an incident report form, before giving a brief recommendation on what the next steps should be.

Witness 1

My name is Henry, and this is what I saw:

At 15:00 today, I was walking out of the sports shop in the Ficshire shopping centre. I'd been there to pick up a new pair of white trainers, which I was going to wear to my friend's birthday party. I'd put them on when I left the shop, because I was fed up of wearing my dad's shoes. As I walked past the escalator, I stopped to look at a sign which was posted on the wall. The sign was talking about achieving justice for a gorilla at the local zoo, which had just been euthanized. I'd read about the story in the local newspaper, but didn't realise it was a big deal. Anyway as I stopped to study it, I noticed two people arguing right next to me. One of them was the local security guard. In his hand, he was holding a pink handbag. He was arguing with a blonde girl, who was claiming that she didn't steal the bag and wanted it back from him. The girl was wearing a blue dress, with white socks and black slip on shoes. I'd say she was quite tall, about five foot 7 or 8, but there was a pretty girl behind her who had brown hair and green eyes; so I wasn't paying too much attention. The security guard didn't seem to believe the girl, and was holding the bag at arms' length. Eventually she started getting really angry and when he radioed for assistance, she smacked him right in the face, from out of nowhere! The girl with brown hair screamed. He dropped the bag and the blonde girl ran off with it. I went over to the security guard to help him, even though really I just wanted to talk to the brown haired girl, and then left the shopping centre at 15:15.

Witness 2

My name is Gemma, and this is what I saw:

At 10 past 3 in the afternoon, I was coming up the escalator to the second floor of the shopping centre. I'd been shopping for some premium dog food, for my two German Shepherds, when I noticed two people arguing. One of the people, the security guard at the shopping centre, was shouting at a girl with blonde hair, in a blue dress. I noticed that she had breadcrumbs all over the front of her dress, and heard her say that her name was Katie. She was about 5 ft 7 in height. There was a girl standing behind her who I used to know from school, and didn't really like very much. I was trying not to make eye contact with her but I definitely think she saw me, even though she was on her phone. Her hair is brown now but it used to be blonde. It looks awful! The blonde girl was politely asking for her pink bag back, and claimed that there had been a mistake. The man just kept shouting at her, and was very aggressive. Eventually, Katie got very frustrated. She punched him in the face, and then ran off with the bag; past the big gorilla sign hanging on the wall. I hadn't noticed that sign before but as someone who goes to the zoo, I was really upset to hear the gorilla had been euthanized. I then left the shopping centre at half past 3.

Witness 3

My name is Josh, and this is what I saw:

At 5 past 3 in the afternoon, I was shopping with my girlfriend in a local handbag store, *Handbags Rock.* We were looking for a cheap handbag for my Mum's birthday. I didn't know what to pick so I'd brought her along to help me out. We had been arguing over the prices all day. I felt that $50 was far too much for a handbag, but she thought we should be spending much more. While arguing, we were stood next to a fairly tall girl in a blue dress, who kept glancing over at the security staff. She was eating a sandwich. At one point she dropped the sandwich, but quickly picked it up again off the floor and resumed eating it. I was studying a nice cheap red handbag; when to the shock of both me and my girlfriend, the blonde girl snatched a handbag off the shelf and ran out of the shop! We couldn't remember if the handbag was red or pink, but we were surprised that no alarms went off. Luckily, a security guard noticed it, and quickly ran after her. He didn't seem very fast though. We dashed outside to see what was happening, and after a few moments of searching, saw the security guard lying on the floor with a bloody nose. The girl was nowhere to be seen. The guard was helped to his feet by a strange looking boy in white trainers, who informed us that a blonde girl had punched him. He kept trying to get the attention of another girl, on the other side of the escalator. It wasn't working. We went directly over and offered to give a statement.

HOW TO ANSWER THIS

When answering this question, you need to take the same approach that we did in the first two questions, whereby the report was written out in clear paragraphs and sentences. At all times, make sure you are paying close attention to the facts. Your recommendation at the end of the exercise counts for only a small proportion of the mark. Do not use information which isn't evident from the passage, and don't include irrelevant details (inserted to throw you off) for example including the fact that Josh thinks $50 is too much for a handbag, or that there was a gorilla sign on the wall.

Below we have included a list of facts from the extract, in a bullet point list. Use textbox below the list to turn these into an incident report form, similar to the previous exercises.

- The incident in question occurred between 10 past 3 and quarter past 3, on the second floor of the Ficshire Shopping Centre, at the top of the escalator.

- A girl, named Katie, was accused by a security guard of stealing a pink handbag from the store *Handbags Rock*.

- The girl was wearing a blue dress, with white socks and black slip on shoes. She had been eating a sandwich and had breadcrumbs on the front of her dress. She had blonde hair and was five foot 7 in height.

- After an argument with the security guard, Katie punched the guard and ran off with the dress. It is not clear whether the security guard behaved aggressively, but it is certain that Katie did behave aggressively in striking him.

- My recommendation would be to examine the CCTV footage of this incident carefully. There should be CCTV both in the shop and in the shopping centre where the alleged incident took place. This will allow us to examine whether the customer did actually steal the bag (in which case her complaint is unfounded) and then take criminal action against her.

VISUAL EXERCISE

The second half of this exercise will be more challenging, and will require you to recognise visual evidence. You will be shown a DVD of an interview between a witness to an incident, and a shop assistant/employee of an effected organisation, and will then be required to create an Incident Report Form based on what was said in the video.

Where the first exercise will challenge you on what it was you read, now you will be challenged on your ability to **listen**. Similarly to the first task, you need to be able to distinguish relevant information from irrelevant, and construct a well written report. The purpose of this exercise is for the assessors to determine whether you are someone who can work accurately under pressure, who will not allow any preconceived judgements or opinions to get in the way of good police work.

Here are some things to look out for during the visual exercise:

-Pay close attention to what the person being interviewed is saying. You will not be given a second watch of the DVD, and therefore you need to glean as much detail from the first watch as possible.

-Watch out for any discrepancies or contradictions. Remember that not all witnesses are reliable, sometimes the witness may contradict themselves. In your report form, you will be given a space for further notes, where you can mention this; however the main body of the report form should only consist of facts.

-Remember that not every witness will be clear in what they are saying. People speak in a variety of different ways, and come from a variety of different backgrounds. You need to try as hard as possible to understand **everyone** who is being interviewed. At times, the interviewer in the DVD should make this easier for you by clarifying certain things.

-This exercise will test your perception of individuals. Remember that police officers are unbiased and never discriminatory. You should treat every single person that you meet in a fair and positive manner.

-Remember that the aim of this exercise isn't to find out whether someone is lying, it's to find out the truth. The people being interviewed aren't suspects, they are witnesses.

Now, take a look at our sample exercise below. The following is a **transcript** of an interview. During the real exercise, you will be required to physically watch a video.

INCIDENT REPORT FORM: EXERCISE 3

The following is a transcript between a shop manager and a witness to an incident that occurred on Ficshire Lane, on 17th July 2015.

The shop manager is named Mr Rodgers, who owns *BuyYourThings* and the employee is Lucas Hill.

....

Mr Rodgers: Thank you for taking the time to see me, Mr Hill.

Lucas Hill: No problem, happy to help.

Mr Rodgers: Now, I understand that you were the witness to a shoplifting incident earlier today, at *BuyYourThings*. Is that right?

Lucas Hill: That's right.

Mr Rodgers: Can you tell me what you saw?

Lucas Hill: Well, at the time I was walking my dog. We took a stroll around Silverdale and I then got home at 12:00. I then headed to the University, where I sell pizza for charity. On my way to the University, I passed your shop. I've been in once or twice before, to pick up some things for my wife. I noticed a man in a hood hanging around suspiciously outside the door. He seemed anxious and was concealing his face. Then, he dashed into the shop. A few seconds later I heard an alarm go off and he ran back out of the door with several items under his arm, jumped into a blue getaway car down the street and was gone.

Mr Rodgers: Do you know what time the man ran into the shop?

Lucas Hill: Ummmm…I would say 12 o'clock but that would be quite illogical, since that's what time I got home. I imagine that I left home at about 20 past 12, so I'd say about half past 12.

Mr Rodgers: Did you notice what items the man stole?

Lucas Hill: I didn't see anything, since he had several things concealed under his shirt and in his navy tracksuit bottoms, but I know that he definitely had a box with a phone in it in his hand. I recognised the logo. That's all though.

Mr Rodgers: What about the getaway car?

Lucas Hill: I believe it was a red ford fiesta.

Mr Rodgers: Right. And did you catch any glimpse of the man's facial features?

Lucas Hill: Not really. He was quite short, probably a good 2 inches shorter than me…and I'm 5 ft 8. So he was probably about 5 ft 4, or 5 ft 5.

Mr Rodgers: Any distinguishing facial qualities?

Lucas Hill: Oh yes…I was quite surprised because he was clean shaven and for some reason I always thought of most criminals as having beards.

Mr Rodgers: You said that he was wearing a hoodie. Did it have a logo on it, or a particular colour? What about his shoes?

Lucas Hill: He was wearing white trainers…the hoodie was black and had a red logo in the chest area.

Mr Rodgers: What happened after the man had escaped from the shop?

Lucas Hill: Well, the first thing I did was rush into the shop to check that everything was okay. The manager at the time, Wendy, was on the phone to the police. Some of the shop shelves and displays had been knocked down in the confusion and there was also some glass on the floor. I immediately set about assisting the shop employees with tidying up the floor.

Mr Rodgers: Did any of them say anything to you about the robbery?

Lucas Hill: Erm...I'm not sure, why?

Mr Rodgers: When an incident such as this occurs, it's important for us to make certain that nobody inside our establishment was involved.

Lucas Hill: No, I don't think so. Or at least, nobody said anything incriminating to me. We just chatted generally about tidying up, and they all made sure to thank me once I left.

Mr Rodgers: Thank you for providing me with all of that information, Mr Hill. As you can guess, the thieves have taken a significant amount of valuable items.

Lucas Hill: Yes, I can imagine that the laptop he stole was quite expensive...

Mr Rodgers: Very. If we need further information, we might contact you again. Are you okay with this?

Lucas Hill: Sure, no problem.

How to answer this

Just as we did in the first exercise, you should take a structured approach to answering this question. Make sure that you establish what facts are relevant, and what facts are irrelevant. For example, we don't need to know that Mr Hill was walking his dog earlier in the day, but we do need to know what he was doing at the time, or what the suspect was wearing. These are **key facts** and are very important to your report.

Now, take a look at our sample response to this question.

SAMPLE RESPONSE

The following has been written in response to the burglary incident that occurred at BuyYourThings, at 12:30 pm, on the 17th July 2015.

On the day in question, Lucas Hill (the witness) was walking to work. On his way through Ficshire Lane, he claims to have noticed a suspicious looking character hanging around outside the shop named BuyYourThings. He describes this character in the following way:

-Male, approximately 5 ft 5, clean shaven, wearing blue tracksuit bottoms, a black hoodie with a red logo and white trainers.

Mr Hill claims that as he walked past the shop, the man ran into the premises, and a few seconds later emerged with several items of value. Mr Hill did not see many of these items, as they were concealed within the man's clothing. However, he claims to have recognised a box containing a phone, and later a laptop. It is notable that Mr Hill contradicts himself on this point, as he earlier states that the only item he saw was the box containing the phone.

Mr Hill then states that the man escaped from the scene in a Blue Ford Fiesta. However, he also contradicts himself on this point, later describing the car as red.

The result of this crime was that several high value items were stolen, and there was significant damage to the shop. Both Mr Hill and Mr Rodgers note that shelves were damaged, shop displays were knocked over and glass was smashed during the robbery. Along with the psychological impact of the crime, and the theft, this amounts to a criminal offence.

Now that you've seen how to go about tackling this type of exercise, have a go at the sample exercise below.

INCIDENT REPORT FORM: EXERCISE 4

The following is a transcript of a conversation between a restaurant owner, and a witness to an incident that occurred on the 18th October, 2014.

The restaurant owner is named Ramshad Siddique, and the witness is named Alicia Brooks.

....

Ramshad: Thank you for agreeing to see me, Mrs Brooks.

Alicia: No problem, I hope I can help.

Ramshad: As you know, there have been a spate of recent graffiti incidents in foreign restaurants around the town.

Alicia: That's right.

Ramshad: I'm led to believe that you witnessed somebody defacing our property an hour ago?

Alicia: I believe so, yes.

Ramshad: Can you tell me exactly what you saw?

Alicia: Well, I work in the jewellers down the road, and walk past your restaurant on my way home for lunch. I was on my way back when I saw somebody with their back to me. I could immediately smell fresh paint, and what sounded like a spraying noise. Upon closer inspection, I realised that the individual with their back to me was spray painting the front of your restaurant window, with what looked like offensive words.

Ramshad: And what did you do next?

Alicia: Well, I was quite torn. If I confronted the person, they might react aggressively, but if I stood back and let them continue then I would be allowing them to break the law. I decided to speak up. Unfortunately, I barely had a time to get out a full sentence before the person dropped their spray paint, pushed me out the way and ran away down the street.

Ramshad: Were you hurt? And did you catch a glimpse of their face?

Alicia: No, I was a little shaken but not hurt. I did get a good view of their face actually, yes. It was a teenage boy, no more than 14 or 15 years old I'd say. He had brown hair, green eyes and a piercing in his left ear.

Ramshad: Can you tell me what he was wearing?

Alicia: He was dressed in black, from head to toe...although his front and trousers were absolutely covered in red spray paint.

Ramshad: That's very useful information. Did the boy say anything to you?

Alicia: He swore when he saw me. He had a distinctive Scottish accent...very gruff.

Ramshad: Right, and as you say this was an hour ago?

Alicia: Yes, at 13:15. I was going to call the police but I thought it would be better to wait for you to get back to survey the damage.

Ramshad: Unfortunately this is not the first such incident. An individual with a similar description has been defacing our property before, but we've never been able to catch them. Luckily now we've got the dropped can of spray paint to use as evidence.

Alicia: The person in question was wearing gloves, so you might struggle to get fingerprints.

Ramshad: Ah, that's a shame. I'm sure it will be useful though. Did you see anything else that you think might be useful? And would you be willing to testify against this person if we took the issue to the police?

Alicia: No, that's all I saw, but yes I'd be very happy to testify if necessary.

Sample Response

FINAL TIPS FOR PASSING THE WRITTEN EXERCISES

- In the build-up to your assessment, practise plenty of report writing.

- Improve your spelling, grammar and punctuation.

- Do not use words that you find hard to spell.

- Make sure your handwriting is neat, tidy and legible.

- Do not spend too long reading the documentation and paperwork that you are provided with. You need to allocate sufficient time to write your report or letter.

When creating your written report or letter, use the documentation provided to make suggestions as to how the situation could be improved or addressed.

I would also strongly recommend that you state the reasons why you have chosen that particular course of action.

Where appropriate, deal with the issue in a constructive manner and always use correct spelling and grammar.

THE ROLE-PLAY/INTERACTIVE EXERCISES

During the police officer assessment centre you will have to deal with four interactive exercises or role plays as they are otherwise called. The type of situation that you will be confronted with varies greatly. However, examples of the types of exercises that have been used in the past include the following:

- A customer of the centre wants to discuss an incident that happened at the centre.

- A shop owner in centre wants to discuss an incident at their shop.

- An employee within the centre has been asked to attend a meeting.

- An employee within the centre has been asked to attend a meeting.

The situation that you will have to deal with is irrelevant. It is how you interact with the role play actor and what you say that is important. You must be able to demonstrate the police officer core competencies during each role-play scenario.

Examples of how you would achieve this include:

- Dealing with the role play actor in a sensitive and supportive manner;

- Having respect for people's views and feelings;

- Seeing issues from others' points of view;

- Ask relevant questions to clarify the situation;

- Listening to people's needs and interests;

- Respecting confidentiality where appropriate;

- Presenting an appropriate image;

- Trying to sort out customers' problems as soon as possible;

- Make reference to any supporting documentation, policies or procedures;

- Confirming that the customer is happy with your offered solution.

- Keeping customers updated on any progress that you

make.

It is crucial that you learn the core competencies and are also able to demonstrate them during each exercise.

This part of the selection process will be split into two five-minute parts. The first part will consist of the preparation phase and the second part will be the actual activity phase that you'll be assessed against. I will now explain each phase in detail.

THE PREPARATION PHASE

During the five-minute preparation phase you will be provided with the actual scenario, either on a card or sheet of paper. You may also be provided with additional documentation that is relevant to the scenario that you'll be required to deal with. You will be taken to a desk or a separate room where you will have just five minutes in which to prepare for the activity phase. During the preparation phase you will be allowed to take notes and then use them during the activity phase. At the end of the activity phase you will normally be required to hand in your notes to the assessor. You will not be permitted to take any writing utensils into the activity phase.

Having personally been through this type of role play assessment I found that by learning the Welcome Pack prior to the assessment day made my life a lot easier. The preparation phase was easy, simply because I knew my role as customer services officer inside out. I knew the code of conduct, the equality policy statement, and all other relevant information that was applicable to my role. As soon as I turned over the role play scenario I knew exactly what I was required to do. Although the preparation phase is not assessable, you must still use the time wisely.

This is how I recommend you use the time:

- Quickly read the scenario and any supporting information/documentation. If you have already studied the Welcome Pack prior to assessment your life will be a lot easier.

- Once you have studied the scenario and any additional information/documentation you should then separate relevant information from irrelevant information, just like you did during the written report writing stage. Write down brief notes as to what you think is relevant.

- You now need to cross match any relevant information from the scenario with procedures, policies and your responsibilities that are provided in the Welcome Pack. For example, if within the scenario it becomes apparent that somebody from the centre is being bullied or harassed, you will need to know, use and make reference to the equality policy statement during the activity phase of the assessment. Another example would be where a child has been reported missing. If this was the case then you would possibly wish to make use of the security guards, the tannoy system and also the CCTV cameras that are based around the centre.

- I would now recommend that you write down on your note paper a step by step approach as what you intend to do during the activity stage. An example of this may be as follows:

STEP 1
**Introduce myself to the role actor
and ask him/her how I can help them.**

(Remember to be polite and respectful and treat the role

play actor in a sensitive and supportive manner. You are being assessed against the core competency of respect for race and diversity during every role play scenario)

STEP 2
Listen to them carefully and ask relevant questions to establish the facts.

(How, When, Where, Why, Who)

STEP 3
Clarify the information received to check you have understood exactly what has happened.

STEP 4
Provide a suitable solution to the problem or situation and tell the role play actor what you intend to do.

(Remember to use keywords and phrases from the core competencies)

STEP 5
**Check to confirm that the role play actor is happy with your solution.
Provide a final summary of what you intend to do and ask them if there is anything else you can help them with.**

(Tell the role actor that you will take responsibility for solving the problem and that you will keep them updated on progress)

Once you have made your notes and created a plan of action you are now ready to go through to the activity phase. Before we move on to this stage of the role play assessment I will provide you with a further explanation of how you may wish to approach the preparation phase using a sample scenario.

SAMPLE ROLE-PLAY EXERCISE 1

You are the customer service manager at a fictitious retail centre. A member of your staff approaches you and tells you that she has been bullied by another member of staff. The woman is clearly upset by the situation and she wants you to take action.

How to prepare

If you have already taken the time to study the Welcome Pack prior to attending the assessment then the first thing that will spring to your mind will be the equality policy statement. Within the statement you will find specific details about how to deal with situations of this nature and it is essential that you follow each step carefully. Remember that one of the assessable core competencies requires you to gather all relevant information (decision making).

Using my 5 step plan the following is how I might deal with this type of situation:

STEP 1 – I would walk into the activity room and introduce myself to the role actor. I would ask them sensitively what the problem was and how I could help them. If there was a chair available in the room then I would ask them to sit down.

STEP 2 – I would listen very carefully to what they had to say and symapthise where appropriate. I would then start to establish the facts of the case asking them relevant questions such as:

- How long had the bullying been going on for?

- Who was involved and what had they been doing/ saying?

- Were any other people involved?

- Have there been any witnesses to this incident?

- Had they asked the other person to stop bullying them and if so what was their reaction?

STEP 3 – I would then clarify and confirm with the role actor that I had gathered the correct facts.

STEP 4 – At this stage I would take full control of the situation and tell the role actor what I intended to do about the situation. I would make reference at this stage to the equality policy statement and I would use it as a basis for solving the problem. I would also use keywords and phrases that matched the core competencies.

STEP 5 – During the final stages of the role play activity stage I would check to confirm that the role play actor is happy with my solution. I would provide them with a final summary of what I intend to do and I would ask them if there is anything else that I would help them with. I would also confirm at this stage that I was going to take responsibility for resolving the problem and that I would keep them updated on progress as and when it occurred.

Once the 5 minute preparation phase is complete a buzzer will sound and you will then move to the activity stage of the assessment.

The activity phase
The activity stage will again last for 5 minutes and it is during this phase that you are required to interact with the role actor.

During the activity stage there will be an assessor in the room whose responsibility it is to assess you against the core competencies. Try to ignore them and concentrate fully on how you interact with the role actor. There may also be a third person in the room who will be there to shadow the assessor or for quality assurance purposes. During the activity stage you will be assessed on what you did and how you did it. You will usually be graded from A to D with the highest score earning you an A to the weakest score earning you a D.

Obviously you want to aim for an A but don't be disheartened if you feel that you haven't done well on a particular exercise, as you can make up your grades in another. If you score a D against the core competency of respect for race and diversity then you will fail the entire assessment.

During the previous sample role play exercise (exercise 1) we focused on a complaint made by a member of staff who claimed that she was being bullied by another member of staff. Within the equality policy statement you will find suggested courses of action. The options here may suggest that the person asks the offender to stop, the problem is discussed with an appropriate person (you) or the option is available to make a formal complaint.

Below I have provided you with some suggested responses to this type of exercise followed by an explanation. Most of these can be applied to similar exercises surrounding harassment cases, although you should judge every situation separately and act according to the brief.

SAMPLE RESPONSES AND ACTIONS TO EXERCISE 1

Response

"Thank you for coming to see me today. I understand that you have a problem with another member of staff?"

Explanation

During this type of response you are demonstrating a level of customer care and you are focusing on the needs of the individual. Remember to use open body language and never become confrontational, defensive or aggressive.

Response

"Would you be able to tell me exactly what has happened and how this has affected you? I will also need to ask you whose been bullying you, where it has been occurring and on how many occasions including dates and times."

Explanation

Again you are focusing on the needs of the individual, which is important. Try to look and sound genuine and also use suitable facial expressions. In order to 'problem solve' you must first ask questions and gather the facts of the incident.

Response

"It must be very difficult for you to bring this matter to my attention; you are to be praised for this course of action."

Explanation

During this response you are demonstrating a caring nature and you are providing a high level of service.

Response
"Have you asked him to stop or have you informed anybody else of this situation?"

and

"Are you aware of this happening to anybody else?"

Explanation
Here you are gathering the facts, which will help you provide a suitable resolution to the problem.

Response
"The company equality policy in relation to this kind of alleged behaviour is quite clear, it states XYZ. It will NOT be tolerated and I can assure you the matter will be dealt with."

Explanation
During this response you are detailing the company equality policy. This demonstrates to the assessor that you are fully aware of the policies and procedures – this will gain you higher scores. You are also stating that this type of behaviour is not accepted and you are, therefore, challenging the inappropriate behaviour in line with the police officer core competencies.

Response
"Before I detail my solution to this problem I want to first of all confirm the details of the case. Please can you confirm that...."

Explanation
During this response I am confirming and checking that the details I have obtained are correct.

Response
"Please be aware that you can make a formal complaint if you so wish? Your feelings and wishes are paramount during my investigation. What would you like to happen from here? Would you like to make a formal complaint against the individual concerned?"

Explanation
By asking the complainant what they want to do, you are demonstrating that you are putting their needs first and you are respecting confidentiality.

Response
"Let me assure you that this matter will be dealt with as a priority but in the meantime I will place another member of staff with you so that you can work in a comfortable environment. Are you happy with this course of action?"

Explanation
Here you are taking action to resolve the problem. You are also informing the person how you intend to resolve it. Finally you are checking that the person is happy with your actions.

Response
"May I thank you again for bringing this matter to my attention; I will keep you fully informed of all progress. I wish to inform you that I will be taking personal responsibility for resolving this issue. Is there anything else I can do for you?"

Explanation
Finally you are demonstrating a high level of service and also checking if there is anything else that you can do for them. You are also taking personal responsibility for resolving the

issue. It is important to tell them that you will keep them informed of the outcome of any investigation.

TOP TIPS FOR PREPARING FOR THE ROLE-PLAY EXERCISES

- Learn the core competencies that are being assessed and be able to 'act' out each one.

- A good way to practice for these exercises is to get a friend or family relative to 'role-play' the sample exercises contained within this guide.

- When practicing the exercises, try to pick someone you know who will make it difficult for you. Also, try to resolve each issue in a calm but effective manner, in line with the core competencies.

- You may wish to purchase a copy of the 'Police Role Play' DVD now available at www.how2become.com.

TOP TIPS FOR PASSING FOR THE ROLE-PLAY EXERCISES

- Use the preparation time wisely.

- Learn the pre assessment material before you go to the assessment. This will make your life much easier.

- Remain calm during every role-play. Even if the actor becomes confrontational, it is essential that you remain calm and in control.

- If at any time during the role play activity phase the role play actor uses language that is either inappropriate (including swearing), discriminatory or uses any form of harassment then you must challenge it immediately. When challenging this kind of behaviour you must do so in an assertive manner without becoming aggressive. Always be polite and respectful at all times.

- Use effective listening skills during the role-play exercises and ask questions in order to gather the facts.

- Once you have gathered the facts of the case or situation then solve the problem.

On the following pages I have provided you with a number of sample role-play exercises. To begin with, read each exercise carefully and then take notes in the box provided detailing how you might deal with the situation. Make sure you have a copy of the core competencies to hand when making your notes.

Next, get a friend or relative to act out each scenario so you can practise dealing with it.

SAMPLE ROLE-PLAY EXERCISE 2

You are the customer services officer at a fictitious retail centre. A school teacher has lost a pupil in the shopping centre and he wants to discuss the matter with you. He is very annoyed that it took him so long to find your office. He states that there were no security staff around and his pupil has now been missing for fifteen minutes.

He wants to know what you intend to do about it.

How to prepare and possible actions

- To begin with, you should study the 'OPERATIONS' information about the centre. What does it say that possibly relates to the above scenario? Is there any CCTV?

- Are there any security staff that could help look for any missing persons?

- Is there a police station within the complex and can the police be used to respond to situations like this?

- Request the attendance of the police immediately.

- Make sure that you keep the teacher in the office with you so that they can provide further information to the police about the missing child.

- Try to gather information about the missing child – How old are they? What are they wearing? What is their name? Are there any distinguishing features? Where were they last seen?

- Try to reassure the teacher that everything will be ok.

- If there is the option of using a loudspeaker system in the shopping centre then this could be used to transmit a 'missing persons' message.

- Consider the option of using the centre's CCTV cameras to locate the missing person.

- Consider positioning a member of the security team at each exit to prevent anybody walking out with the child.

On the following page I have provided a sample response to this exercise. Read it before using the box on the following page to take notes on how you would deal with this situation.

Sample responses and actions to exercise 2

"Hello sir, my name is Richard and I'm the customer service manager for this centre. I understand that one of your pupils has gone missing in the centre – is that correct?" (Establish exactly what has happened).

"Firstly can I reassure you that the police have been called and they are on their way. I have also put a security guard at each exit to look out for the missing child. In the meantime I would like to take some notes from you.

Please can you give me a full description of the missing pupil please including their name?" (Make a list of the description.)

"Please can you tell me how long ago they have been missing for and where they were last seen?"

"Have you or anybody else been looking for the missing person and have you reported this to anybody else yet?"

"Is there a possibility that they might have wandered off to their favourite shop or gone somewhere else with another parent who was in the group?"

"Do you think they would understand their own name if we broadcast this over the loudspeaker system?"

"OK Sir, thank you for providing me with these details. This is what I propose to do in order to resolve the situation. To begin with I will check the CCTV cameras to see if we can locate the missing child. I will also brief all members of staff at the centre, including the security guards, of the missing child's description. I will also put out a tannoy announcement asking the missing child to go to the nearest customer services desk where a member of staff will meet them."

"In addition to this course of action I will also put the registered

nurse on standby so that she can treat the child for shock if appropriate."

"In the meantime please stay here until the police arrive, as it is important you provide them with more information. Let me reassure you that we will do everything we possibly can to locate the missing person. I will be taking personal responsibility for resolving this issue and I will keep you updated on progress as and when it occurs."

Notes for sample role-play exercise 2

SAMPLE ROLE-PLAY EXERCISE 3

You are the customer services officer at a fictitious retail centre. One of the centre shop managers wants to see you about a gang of youths who are standing outside his shop behaving in an anti-social manner, swearing and obstructing customers from entering his shop. He is very annoyed at the situation and is losing money because potential customers are not allowed to shop in comfort without feeling threatened.

How to prepare and possible actions

- To begin with you should study the 'OPERATIONS' information and the 'CODE OF CONDUCT' information in the Welcome Pack. What do they say that possibly relates to the above scenario? Is this kind of behaviour tolerated? Can people who behave in such a manner be escorted from the centre and should the police be involved? Can you involve the security staff or use the CCTV cameras to provide the police with evidence?

- Remember that the manager is annoyed at the situation and therefore you may have to diffuse a confrontational situation in the first instance. Remember to be firm but stay calm and never become confrontational yourself.

On the following page I have provided a sample response to this exercise. Read it before using the box on the following page to take notes on how you would deal with this situation.

Sample responses and actions to exercise 3

"Hello Sir, thank you for coming to see me today. My name is Richard and I am the customer services officer at the centre. I understand there is an issue with a gang of youths outside your shop?" (Establish the facts of the incident by asking relevant questions).

"Can I first of all say that I fully understand how frustrating this must be for you as you are losing customers all the time the problem is present. I wish to apologise unreservedly for any problems that you are experiencing at the centre. I have called the police and they are on their way. In the meantime it is important that I take into consideration your feelings and opinions. Therefore, please can you provide me with some information about what has been happening?" (Make a list of what has happened.)

"How many people are there outside your shop? Has this happened before or is this the first time?"

"Have you reported it to anyone else? Can you provide me with a description of the people who are creating the problem? What type of language are they using?"

"May I reassure you Sir that in line with the code of conduct at the centre will not tolerate any form of anti-social behaviour and we have the power to remove people from the building and prevent them from re-entering at a later point. Whilst we await the arrival of the police I will try to see if the CCTV cameras have picked up anything."

"I am sorry that you have had to go through this experience Sir but we will do everything we can to rectify the problem. As the customer services officer for the centre it is my responsibility to ensure you receive the highest standard of customer care. With that in mind I will be taking full responsibility for resolving this issue and I will keep you updated of all progress as and when it occurs. Is there anything else I can help you with?"

Notes for sample role-play exercise 3

SAMPLE ROLE-PLAY EXERCISE 4

A customer would like to see you about an issue surrounding a dog that is in the shopping centre. She is very annoyed that a dog has been allowed to enter the shopping centre and wants to know what you are going to do about it. The dog is an 'assistance dog' for a visually impaired customer.

How to prepare and possible actions

- To begin with you should study the 'OPERATIONS' information, the 'CODE OF CONDUCT' information and the 'EQUALITY POLICY' statement relating to the centre. What do they say that possibly relates to the above scenario? Are 'assistance dogs' permitted? If the answer is 'yes' then the person may not have any grounds for complaint. However, it is important to listen to the complaint before responding in a calm but firm manner.

- Remember to be confident in your handling of the situation and refer to the policy of the centre for such issues. Do not get drawn into personal opinions but stick to the code of conduct for the centre and apply it accordingly.

On the following page I have provided a sample response to this exercise. Read it before using the box on the following page to take notes on how you would deal with this situation.

Sample responses and actions to exercise 4

"Hello Madam, my name is Richard and I am the customer services officer for the centre, thank you for coming to see me today. I understand there is an issue with a dog in the shopping centre. Please would you explain what the problem is?"

Listen to the customer's complaint and choose an appropriate moment to respond. If at any time the customer uses inappropriate or discriminatory language then you must challenge it in an appropriate manner. It is important that you ask relevant questions in order to establish the facts of the case.

"Whilst dogs are not permitted in the shopping centre, there is an exception for 'assistance dogs' like the one you have just described. Our code of conduct states that assistance dogs for the visually impaired are permitted in the centre. The centre will not discriminate against persons with disabilities and we will do everything we can to help their shopping experience to be a pleasurable one."

"We have a legal requirement to allow 'assistance dogs' into the centre and if we were to ignore these rules we would be in contravention of those laws. I am sorry Madam but in this instance I am unable to take any action. Thank you for coming to see me and have a good day."

Notes for sample role-play exercise 4

ADDITIONAL NOTES AND GUIDANCE

- Please note that the sample scenarios provided within this guide are examples only and they will not be the ones that you are assessed against during the assessment centre. Whilst some of them may be similar you must treat each case based the information provided and the facts surrounding the scenario. It is not the scenario that is important but how you deal with it.

- Remember, never to get annoyed or show signs of anger during the interactive exercises.

- The members of staff who are carrying out the fictitious roles may try to make the situation difficult to deal with. They may come across in a confrontational manner during the role-play scenarios so be prepared for this. Don't let it put you on the back foot and remember that they are trying to test your ability to diffuse confrontational situations. You must remain in control at all times and treat the role actor in a sensitive and supportive manner.

- Most importantly, make sure you remember to respect equality and diversity at all times. You will be assessed in this area during every scenario.

- Challenge any inappropriate behaviour immediately during the role-play scenarios. Be firm where appropriate but do not become confrontational.

- Use keywords and phrases from the core competencies where possible.

- Finally, remember to be confident and firm whenever required. However, do respect your role as a customer service manager and provide a high level of service.

Golden tips

- Always try to deal with the role actor in a sensitive and supportive manner.

- During the role play activity phase ask appropriate questions in order to gather information surrounding the case.

- Once you have gathered your information you must clarify.

- Explain any relevant documentation in your responses. This will gain you higher marks.

- Make sensible suggestions on how you think you can improve the situation.

- Always interact with the role play actor in a clear and constructive manner.

- Be sure to deal with the issues directly in accordance with the Welcome Pack and any other documentation provided.

WANT MORE TEST QUESTIONS?

To obtain more test questions for the police officer selection process please either go to www.how2become.com or search for 'how2become' at Amazon.co.uk.

Attend a 1-Day Police Officer course run by former Police Officers at:

www.PoliceCourse.co.uk

CHAPTER 5

The Police Officer Interview (Assessment Centre)

As part of the police officer assessment centre you will normally be required to sit an interview that is based around the core competencies. Under normal circumstances the interview board will consist of two or three people. These can be from either the uniformed side of the service or support staff.

It is important to remember that whilst you will be nervous you should try not to let this get in the way of your success. Police officers, in general, are confident people who have the ability to rise to a challenge and perform under difficult and pressurised situations. Treat the interview no differently to this. You ARE capable of becoming a police officer and the nerves that you have on the day are only natural, in fact they will help you to perform better if you have prepared sufficiently. The crucial element to your success, as with the rest of the selection process, is your preparation.

The police interview board will have a number of set questions to choose from and, whilst these are constantly changing, they will usually form part of the police officer core competencies. Before attending your interview ensure that you read, digest and understand the police core competencies. Without these it will be difficult to pass the interview.

The interview will last for up to 20 minutes and will ask you four questions about how you have dealt with specific situations in the past. These questions will be related to the competency areas relevant to the role of a Police Officer, which we have shown you earlier in this guide.

They will give you up to five minutes to answer each question. The person interviewing you will stop you if you go over the five minutes. As the person interviewing you asks you the question, they will also give you a written copy of the question to refer to. They may ask you further questions to help you to give a full response. When you consider your responses to the interview questions, you should only choose examples that you feel comfortable discussing with the person interviewing you.

The person who interviews you will assess your responses against the type of behaviours you need to perform effectively in the role. You must make sure that you are familiar with the competencies and that your answer gives you an opportunity to explain how you have shown this behaviour.

They will assess you on five different competencies during the interview. Oral Communication will also be assessed throughout the interview and you will be asked one question in relation to the following four competency areas:

- Service Delivery

- Serving the Public

- Professionalism

- Working with Others

IMPORTANT NOTE:
From time-to-time the police will change the competencies being assessed during the interview. You can find the exact ones being assessed at your particular interview within the **Information for Candidates** documentation.

PREPARING FOR THE ASSESSMENT CENTRE INTERVIEW

When preparing for the assessment centre competency based interview you should try to formulate responses to questions that surround the assessable core competencies. The responses that you provide should be specific examples of where you have been in that particular scenario.

In your 'welcome pack', which will be sent to you approximately 2 weeks before the date of your assessment centre, you should find examples of the 'core competencies' relevant to a police officer. These are the criteria that you will be scored against so it is worthwhile reading them beforehand and trying to structure your answers around them as best you can. For example, one of the sections you will be assessed against could be 'Working with Others'. You may be asked a question where you have to give an example of where you worked effectively as part of a team in order to achieve a difficult task or goal. Try to think of an example where you have had to do this and structure your answer around the core competencies required, e.g. you worked cooperatively with the others, supported the rest of the team members and persuaded them to follow your ideas for completing the task.

On the following page I have provided you with an example of how your response could be structured if you were responding to a question that was based around the core competency of **professionalism**.

Remember that the following sample question and response is for example purposes only.

SAMPLE INTERVIEW QUESTION BASED AROUND THE CORE COMPETENCY OF PROFESSIONALISM.

Question – Please provide an example of where you have taken responsibility to resolve a problem?

"After reading an appeal in my local paper from a local charity I decided to try to raise money for this worthwhile cause by organising a charity car wash day at the local school during the summer holidays. I decided that the event would take place in a month's time, which would give me enough time to organise such an event. The head teacher at the school agreed to support me during the organisation of the event and provide me with the necessary resources required to make it a success.

I set about organising the event and soon realised that I had made a mistake in trying to arrange everything on my own, so I arranged for two of my work colleagues to assist me. Once they had agreed to help me I started out by providing them with a brief of what I wanted them to do. I informed them that, in order for the event to be a success, we needed to act with integrity and professionalism at all times. I then asked one of them to organise the booking of the school and arrange local sponsorship in the form of buckets, sponges and car wash soap to use on the day, so that we did not have to use our own personal money to buy them. I asked the second person to arrange advertising in the local newspaper and radio stations so that we could let the local community know about our charity car wash event, which would in turn hopefully bring in more money on the day for the charity.

Following a successful advertising campaign, I was inundated with calls from local newspapers about our event and it was becoming hard work having to keep talking to them and explaining what the event was all about. But I knew that this information was important if we were to raise our target of £500.

Everything was going well right up to the morning of the event, when I realised we had not got the key to open the school gates. It was the summer holidays so the caretaker was not there to open the gates for us. Not wanting to let everyone down, I jumped in my car and made my way down to the caretaker's house and managed to wake him up and get the key just in time before the car wash event was due to start. In the end the day was a great success and we all managed to raise £600 for the local charity. Throughout the event I put in lots of extra effort in order to make it a great success.

Once the event was over I decided to ask the head teacher for feedback on how he thought I had managed the project. He provided me with some excellent feedback and some good pointers for how I might improve in the future when organising events. I took on-board his feedback in order to improve my skills."

Now that we have taken a look at a sample response, let's explore how the response matched the core competency.

HOW THE RESPONSE MATCHES THE CORE COMPETENCY BEING ASSESSED

In order to demonstrate how effective the above response is I have broken it down into sections and provided the core competency area that it matches.

Sentence
"…I decided to try to raise money for this worthwhile cause by organising a charity car wash day…"

Core competency matched
- Acts with integrity.

- Uses own initiative.

Sentence
"Once they had agreed to help me I started out by providing them with a brief of what I wanted them to do. I informed them that, in order for the event to be a success, we needed to act with integrity and professionalism at all times."

Core competency matched
- Acting with integrity and demonstrating a strong work ethic.

Sentence
"...which would give me enough time to organise such an event."

Core competency matched
- Takes ownership.

Sentence
"I set about organising the event and soon realised that I had made a mistake in trying to arrange everything on my own, so I arranged for 2 of my work colleagues to assist me."

Core competency matched
- Takes ownership.

- Uses initiative.

Sentence
"...arrange local sponsorship in the form of buckets, sponges and car wash soap to use on the day, so that we did not have to use our own personal money to buy them."

Core competency matched

- Uses initiative.

Sentence

"Once the event was over I decided to ask the head teacher for feedback on how he thought I had managed the project. He provided me with some excellent feedback and some good pointers for how I might improve in the future when organising events. I took on-board his feedback in order to improve my skills."

Core competency matched

- Asks for and acts on feedback.

Sentence

"Following a successful advertising campaign, I was inundated with calls from local newspapers about our event and it was becoming hard work having to keep talking to them and explaining what the event was all about. But I knew that this information was important if we were to raise our target of £500."

Core competency matched

- Uses initiative.

Sentence

"Not wanting to let everyone down, I jumped in my car and made my way down to the caretaker's house and managed to wake him up and get the key just in time before the car wash event was due to start."

Core competency matched

- Uses initiative.

- Takes ownership.

- Showing a strong work ethic.

The explanations above have hopefully highlighted the importance of matching the core competencies that are being assessed.

When you receive your 'Welcome Pack', make sure you read it thoroughly and prepare yourself fully for the interview. Preparation is everything and by reading exactly what is required you will increase your chances of success on the day.

On the following pages I have provided you with a number of sample assessment centre interview questions that are based around the core competencies. Following each question we have provided you with some useful tips and advice on how you may consider answering the question.

Once you have read the question and the tips, use the template on the following page to create a response using your own experiences and knowledge.

SAMPLE COMPETENCY BASED INTERVIEW QUESTION 1 (WORKING WITH OTHERS)

Please provide an example of where you have worked as part of a team to achieve a difficult task.

Tips for constructing your response

- Try to think of a situation where you volunteered to work with a team in order to achieve a difficult task. It is better to say that you volunteered as opposed to being asked to get involved by another person.

- Those candidates who can provide an example where they achieved the task despite the constraints of time will generally score better.

- Consider structuring your response in the following manner:

STEP 1 Explain what the situation was and how you became involved.

STEP 2 Now explain who else was involved and what the task was.

STEP 3 Explain why the task was difficult and whether there were any time constraints.

STEP 4 Explain how it was decided who would carry out what task.

STEP 5 Now explain what had to be done and how you overcame any obstacles or hurdles.

STEP 6 Explain what the result/outcome was. Try to make the result positive as a result of your actions.

Now use the template on the following page to construct your own response to this question based on your own experiences and knowledge.

Sample competency based interview question 1

Please provide an example of where you have worked as part of a team to achieve a difficult task.

Examples of probing questions

1. Would you have done anything different next time?

2. How did the end result make you feel?

SAMPLE COMPETENCY BASED INTERVIEW QUESTION 2 (PROFESSIONALISM)

Provide an example of where you have challenged someone's behaviour that was either discriminatory or inappropriate. What did you do and what did you say?

Tips for constructing your response

- Read carefully the core competency that relates to respect for race and diversity before constructing your response.

- When challenging this type of behaviour, make sure you remain calm at all times and never become aggressive or confrontational.

- Consider structuring your response in the following manner:

STEP 1 Explain what the situation was and how you became involved.

STEP 2 Now explain who else was involved and why you felt that the behaviour was inappropriate or discriminatory. What was it that was being said or done?

STEP 3 Now explain what you said or did and why.

STEP 4 Explain how the other person/people reacted when you challenged the behaviour.

STEP 5 Now explain what the end result was. Try to make the result positive following your actions.

STEP 6 Finally explain why you think it was that the people/person behaved as they did.

Now use the template on the following page to construct your own response to this question based on your own experiences and knowledge.

Sample competency based interview question 2

Provide an example of where you have challenged someone's behaviour that was either discriminatory or inappropriate. What did you do and what did you say?

Examples of probing questions

1. How did you feel when you were challenging their behaviour?

2. How did the person or people react when you challenged their behaviour?

SAMPLE COMPETENCY BASED INTERVIEW QUESTION 3 (WORKING WITH OTHERS)

Provide an example of where you have helped somebody from a different culture or background to your own. What did you do and what did you say?

Tips for constructing your response

- Read carefully the core competency that relates to respect for race and diversity before constructing your response.

- Try to think of a situation where you have gone out of your way to help somebody.

- Try to use keywords and phrases from the core competency in your response.

- Consider structuring your response in the following manner:

STEP 1 Explain what the situation was and how you became involved. It is better to say that you volunteered to be involved rather than to say that you were asked to.

STEP 2 Now explain who else was involved and why they needed your help or assistance?

STEP 3 Now explain what you said or did and why. Also explain any factors you took into consideration when helping them.

STEP 4 Explain how the other person/people reacted to your help or assistance. Did they benefit from it?

STEP 5 Now explain what the end result was. Try to make the result positive following your actions.

Now use the template on the following page to construct your own response to this question based on your own experiences and knowledge.

Sample competency based interview question 3

Provide an example of where you have helped somebody from a different culture or background to your own. What did you do and what did you say?

Examples of probing questions

1.   What did you learn from this experience?

2.   Would you have done anything differently?

SAMPLE COMPETENCY BASED INTERVIEW QUESTION 4 (PROFESSIONALISM)

Provide an example of where you have solved a difficult problem. What did you do?

Tips for constructing your response

- Read carefully the core competency that relates to problem solving.

- Try to include keywords and phrases from the core competency in your response to this question.

- Consider structuring your response in the following manner:

STEP 1 Explain what the situation was and why the problem was difficult.

STEP 2 Now explain what action you took in order to solve the difficult problem?

STEP 3 Now explain why you took that particular action, and also the thought process behind your actions.

STEP 4 Explain the barriers or difficulties that you had to overcome?

STEP 5 Now explain what the end result was. Try to make the result positive following your actions.

Now use the template on the following page to construct your own response to this question based on your own experiences and knowledge.

Sample competency based interview question 4

Provide an example of where you have solved a difficult problem. What did you do?

Examples of probing questions

1. What did you learn from this experience?

2. Could you have done it any better?

SAMPLE COMPETENCY BASED INTERVIEW QUESTION 5 (SERVING THE PUBLIC)

Provide an example of where you have broken down barriers between a group of people?

Tips for constructing your response

- Read carefully the core competency that relates to serving the public.

- Try to include keywords and phrases from the core competency in your response to this question, such as:

  "I tried to understand each person's needs and concerns."

  "I took steps to identify the best way that we could all work together."

  "I had their best interests at heart throughout."

  "I built confidence in them by talking to them."

- Consider structuring your response in the following manner:

STEP 1 Explain what the situation was and why you needed to break down the barriers.

STEP 2 Now explain what steps you took in order to achieve the goal.

STEP 3 Now explain why you took that particular action, and also the thought process behind your actions.

STEP 4 Explain the barriers or difficulties that you had to overcome in order to achieve the task/objective?

STEP 5 Now explain what the end result was. Try to make the result positive following your actions.

Now use the template on the following page to construct your own response to this question based on your own experiences and knowledge.

Sample competency based interview question 5

Provide an example of where you have broken down barriers between a group of people?

Examples of probing questions

1. What did you learn from this experience and would you do anything differently next time?

2. What did the other people think about what you did? Were they happy with your work?

SAMPLE COMPETENCY BASED INTERVIEW QUESTION 6 (SERVICE DELIVERY)

Please provide an example of where you have organised a difficult task effectively?

Tips for constructing your response

- Read carefully the core competency that relates to service delivery.

- Try to include keywords and phrases from the core competency in your response to this question.

- Consider structuring your response in the following manner:

STEP 1 Explain what the situation was and what it was you needed to organise.

STEP 2 Now explain why the task was so difficult.

STEP 3 Now explain what you did and why you did it. Also explain your considerations when organising the task.

STEP 4 Explain what problems you had and how you overcame them.

STEP 5 Finally explain what the end result was. Try to provide a positive outcome to the situation.

Now use the template on the following page to construct your own response to this question based on your own experiences and knowledge.

Sample competency based interview question 6

Please provide an example of where you have organised a difficult task effectively?

Examples of probing questions

1. What did you learn from this experience and would you do anything differently next time?

2. Why do you think the task was so difficult?

SAMPLE COMPETENCY BASED INTERVIEW QUESTION 7 (PROFESSIONALISM)

Tell me about a time when you changed how you did something in response to feedback from someone else?

Tips for creating your response

- What did you need to develop?

- What feedback did you receive and from whom?

- What steps did you take to improve yourself or someone else?

- What did you specifically say or do?

- What was the result?

Strong response

Police officers receive feedback from their supervisory managers on a regular basis. In their quest to continually improve, the Police Service will invest time, finances and resources into your development. Part of the learning process includes being able to accept feedback and also being able to improve as a result of it. Strong performing candidates will be able to provide a specific example of where they have taken feedback from an employer or otherwise, and used it to improve themselves.

Weak response

Those candidates who are unable to accept feedback from others and change as a result will generally provide a weak response to this type of question. They will fail to grasp the importance of feedback and in particular where it lies in relation to continuous improvement. Their response will be generic in nature and there will be no real substance or detail to their answer.

Sample response

"During my last appraisal, my line manager identified that I needed to improve in a specific area. I work as a call handler for a large independent communications company. Part of my role involves answering a specific number of calls per hour. If I do not reach my target then this does not allow the company to meet its standards. I found that I was falling behind on the number of calls answered and this was identified during the appraisal. I needed to develop my skills in the manner in which I handled the call. My line manager played back a number of recorded calls that I had dealt with and it was apparent that I was taking too long speaking to the customer about issues that were irrelevant to the call itself. Because I am conscientious and caring person I found myself asking the customer how they were and what kind of day they were having. Despite the customers being more than pleased with level of customer care, this approach was not helping the company and therefore I needed to change my approach. I immediately took on-board the comments of my line manager and also took up the offer of development and call handling training. After the training, which took two weeks to complete, I was meeting my targets with ease This in turn helped the company to reach it's call handling targets."

Now take the time to use the space that follows to prepare your own response to this question.

Sample competency based interview question 6

Tell me about a time when you changed how you did something in response to feedback from someone else?

Examples of probing questions

1. How did you feel when the feedback was being given?

2. What, if anything, did you find difficult about making the necessary improvements?

MORE SAMPLE QUESTIONS TO PREPARE FOR BASED ON THE ASSESSABLE CORE COMPETENCIES

In this short section I will provide you with a number of sample interview questions to prepare for.

SERVICE DELIVERY

Q. Give an example of when you have worked towards an organisations objectives or priorities?

Q. Give an example of when you have planned and organised a difficult task?

Q. Give an example of when you have carried out many different tasks at once?

Q. Give me an example of when you have sought advice from others whilst carrying out a difficult work-related task?

SERVING THE PUBLIC

Q. Give an example of when you have provided excellent customer service?

Q. Give me an example of when you have addressed someone else's needs or expectations?

Q. Give me an example of when you have broken down barriers amongst a group of people?

Q. Give an example of when you have worked with another person or group of people to deliver an excellent level of service?

PROFESSIONALISM

Q. Give an example of when you have worked in accordance with an organisations standards or ethics?

Q. Give an example of when you have taken ownership of a particular problem?

Q. Give an example of when you have acted on your own initiative to resolve an issue or difficult problem?

Q. Give an example of when you have challenged someone's behaviour which was discriminatory of inappropriate?

Q. Give an example of when you have acted on feedback which has been supplied by someone else?

Q. Give me an example of when you have resolved a difficult situation in a calm manner?

Q. Give me an example of when you have defused a potentially hostile situation?

WORKING WITH OTHERS

Q. Give an example of when you have supported other members of a team?

Q. Give an example of when you have worked with other people to achieve a difficult task?

Q. Give an example of when you have briefed a team in relation to a difficult task which had to be achieved?

Q. Give an example of when you have persuaded a group of people to follow your course of action or plan?

Q. Give an example of when you have treated a person or group of people with dignity and respect?

HOW TO IMPROVE YOUR SCORES THROUGH EFFECTIVE ORAL COMMUNICATION

Whilst you will not normally be questioned directly in relation to oral communication during the interview, you will be assessed indirectly.

During the assessment centre competency-based interview, the panel will be looking to see how you communicate and also how you structure your responses to the interview questions.

Consider the following points both during the interview and whilst responding to the interview questions:

- When you walk into the interview room stand up straight and introduce yourself. Be polite and courteous at all times and try to come across in a pleasant manner. The panel will be assessing you as soon as you walk through the door so make sure you make a positive first impression.

- Do not sit down in the interview chair until you are invited to do so. This is good manners.

- When you sit down in the interview chair, sit up straight and do not fidget or slouch. It is acceptable to use hand gestures when explaining your responses to the questions but don't overdo it, as they can become a distraction.

- Structure your responses to the questions in a logical manner – this is very important. When responding to an interview question, start at the beginning and work your way through in a concise manner, and at a pace that is easy for the panel to listen to.

- Speak clearly and in a tone that is easy for the panel to

hear. Be confident in your responses.

- When talking to the panel use eye contact but be careful not to look at them in an intimidating manner.

- Consider wearing some form of formal outfit to the interview such as a suit. Whilst you will not be assessed on the type of outfit you wear to the interview, it will make you come across in a more professional manner.

Final golden interview tips

- Always provide 'specific' examples to the questions being asked.

- During your responses try to outline your contributions and also provide evidence of the competency area that is being assessed.

- Speak clearly, use correct English and structure their responses in a logical and concise manner.

CHAPTER 6

*The Police Officer
final interview*

Some Police Services have started to introduce what is called a final interview. The final interview is in addition to the assessment centre competency-based interview and will take on a different format.

Within this section of the guide I have provided you with some insider tips and advice on how to prepare for the interview, the type of questions that you may be asked, and also how to respond to them.

To begin with, let's take a look at a few more details relating to the final interview.

ABOUT THE INTERVIEW

The interview will usually take place at the service's training centre or a similar establishment. The purpose of the final interview is to allow the service to ask you questions that are outside of the competencies that have been assessed at the assessment centre. In essence it allows the service to find out more about you, your application, your motivations for wanting to become a police officer, and what you know about the role and the service that you are applying to join. They may also ask you questions that are based around what you might do in a given situation.

The interview panel will normally consist of 2-3 people and is usually made up of uniformed police officers and also a member of the human resources team. The length of the interview will very much depend on the questions the panel want to ask you and also how long your responses are. In general terms the interview will normally last for approximately one hour.

HOW TO PREPARE FOR THE FINAL INTERVIEW

If you have made it this far in the selection process then you have done tremendously well. The Police Service are certainly interested in recruiting you but they want to find out more about you first. There are a number of areas that you will need to prepare for and these are as follows:

1. Interview technique.

2. The reasons why you want to become a police officer and what you know about the role.

3. What you know about the service you are applying to join.

4. Situational interview questions.

Now that we understand how to prepare for the interview, let us break down each particular section in detail.

INTERVIEW TECHNIQUE

Many candidates spend little or no time improving or developing their interview technique. It is important that you spend sufficient time on this area, as it will allow your confidence to improve.

The way to improve interview technique is to carry out what we call a mock interview. Mock interviews are where you ask a friend or relative to ask you a number of interview questions under formalised interview conditions. This can be achieved at home across your dining room table or even whilst sat on the chairs in your living room.

During the mock interview you should work on your interview

technique. The mock interview will also give you a valuable opportunity to try out your responses to a number of sample interview questions that are contained within this guide. It is important that your mock interviewer provides you with constructive feedback. Do not choose somebody who will tell you that you were great, even when you weren't, as this just defeats the whole purpose of a mock interview.

CARRYING OUT A MOCK INTERVIEW

- Choose a quiet room in the house or at another suitable location.

- Set the room up with a table and two chairs.

- The interviewer then invites you into the room and the interview commences. Don't forget to be polite and courteous to the interviewer and only sit down when invited to do so.

- When the interviewer asks you the questions, respond to them in a logical manner and in a tone of voice that can be easily heard.

- Throughout the mock interview work hard on your technique and style. Sit upright at all times and look at the interviewer using soft eye contact. Do not fidget or slouch in the interview chair.

- Once the interview is over, ask the interviewer for feedback on your performance.

- Repeat the process at least three times until you are comfortable with your technique and style of answering.

THE REASONS WHY YOU WANT TO BECOME A POLICE OFFICER AND WHAT YOU KNOW ABOUT THE ROLE

During the final interview the panel may ask you questions that relate to why you want to become a police officer and in particular what you know about the role.

Why do you want to become a police officer?

In the build-up to your interview you need to think carefully about why you want to become a police officer and what it is exactly that has attracted you to the role. Those candidates who want to become a police officer so that they can 'catch criminals' and 'ride about in a police car with the blue lights flashing' will score poorly. Only you will know the exact reasons why you want to join the police but here are some examples of good reasons, and examples of poor reasons.

Good reasons to give

- To make a difference to your community, make it a safer place and reduce any fear that the public may have.

- To carry out a job that is worthwhile and one that makes a difference.

- The variety of the job and the different challenges that you will face on a day-to-day basis.

- The chance to work with a highly professional team that is committed to achieving the values and principles of the service.

- The opportunity to learn new skills.

Poor reasons to give

- The pay and pension.

- The leave or holiday that you will get.

- Wearing a uniform, which ultimately means you don't have to pay for your own work clothes.

- Catching criminals and driving a police car.

What do you know about the role?

After studying this guide you will know a considerable amount about the role of a police officer. Before the final interview you must carry out plenty of research into the role and what the service will expect of you as a serving police officer.

Remember that the role is predominantly based around the core competencies, so be fully familiar with them before you attend the interview. It is also advisable that you study your recruitment literature and also the website of the service you are applying to join.

WHAT YOU KNOW ABOUT THE SERVICE YOU ARE APPLYING TO JOIN

During the final interview there is a strong possibility that you will be asked questions that relate to the service you are applying to join.

The following sample questions are the types that have been asked during final interviews in the past:

Q. What is it that has attracted you to this particular constabulary?

Q. What can you tell me about the structure of this constabulary?

Q. What can you tell me about the geographical area of this Police Service?

Q. Can you tell me how this constabulary is doing in relation to crime reduction?

Q. What crime reduction activities is this constabulary currently involved in?

Q. What is neighbourhood policing and how does this constabulary approach it?

Q. What are the ambitions of this Police Service?

Q. Who are our partners and stakeholders?

In order to prepare for questions that relate to the service you are applying to join, your first port of call is their website. From here you will be able to find out a considerable amount of information about their structure and activities and their success in driving down crime.

You may also wish to consider contacting your local police station and asking if it is possible to talk to a serving police officer about his or her role and the activities that the service are currently engaged in.

SITUATIONAL INTERVIEW QUESTIONS

During the final interview the panel may ask you questions that relate to how you would respond or act in a given situation. This type of question is called a 'situational' type question.

Your response to each situational question must be 'specific' in nature. This means that you must provide an example where you have already been in this type of situation. During your response you should provide details of how you handled or dealt with the situation, preferably with a successful outcome.

Do not fall into the trap of providing a 'generic' response that details what you 'would do' if the situation arose, unless of course you have not been in this type of situation before.

When responding to situational questions try to structure your responses in a logical and concise manner. The way to achieve this is to use the 'STAR' method of interview question response construction:

Situation
Start off your response to the interview question by explaining what the 'situation' was and who was involved.

Task
Once you have detailed the situation, explain what the 'task' was, or what needed to be done.

Action
Now explain what 'action' you took, and what action others took. Also explain why you took this particular course of action.

Result

Explain to the panel what you would do differently if the same situation arose again. It is good to be reflective at the end of your responses. This demonstrates a level of maturity and it will also show the panel that you are willing to learn from every experience.

Finally, explain what the outcome or result was following your actions and those of others. Try to demonstrate in your response that the result was positive because of the action you took.

Now that we have looked into how to prepare for the final interview, it is time to provide you with a number of sample questions and answers. Please note that the questions provided here are for practice purposes only and are not to be relied upon to be the exact questions that you will be asked during your final interview.

Sample final interview questions and sample responses

SAMPLE QUESTION NUMBER 1

Tell us why you want to become a police officer?

Sample response

"I have worked in my current role now for a number of years. I have an excellent employer and enjoy working for them but unfortunately no longer find my job challenging. I understand that the role of a police officer is both demanding and rewarding and I believe I have the qualities to thrive in such an environment. I love working under pressure, working as part of a team that is diverse in nature and helping people in difficult situations. The public expectations of the police are very high and I believe I have the right qualities to help the police deliver the right service to the community.

I have studied the police core competencies and believe that I have the skills to match them and deliver what they require."

Top tips

- Don't be negative about your current or previous employer.

- Be positive, enthusiastic and upbeat in your response.

- Make reference to the core competencies if possible.

SAMPLE QUESTION NUMBER 2

Why have you chosen this particular Police Service?

Sample response

"I have carried out extensive research into the Police Service and in particular this constabulary. I have been impressed by the level of service it provides. The website provides the community with direct access to a different range of topics and the work that is being carried out through your community wardens is impressive. I have looked at the national and local crime statistics and read many different newspapers and articles.

I like this Police Service because of its reputation and the police officers that I have spoken to have told me that they get a great deal of job satisfaction from working here."

Top tips

- Research the service thoroughly and make reference to particular success stories that they have achieved.

- Be positive, enthusiastic and upbeat in your response.

- Be positive about their service and don't be critical of it, even if you think it needs improving in certain areas.

SAMPLE QUESTION NUMBER 3

What does the role of a police officer involve?

Sample response

"Before I carried out my research and looked into the role of the police officer, I had the normal, stereotypical view of a police officer in that they catch criminals and reduce crime for a living.

Whilst there is an element of that in the job, the police officer's role is far more diverse and varied. For example, they are there to serve the community and reduce the element of fear. They do this by communicating with their communities and being visual wherever possible.

They may need to pay particular attention to a person or groups of people who are the victims of crime or hatred. Therefore the role of a police officer is to both physically and psychologically protect the community that they are serving.

It is also their role to work with other organisations such as the Fire Service, Social Services and other public sector bodies to try to reduce crime in a coordinated response as opposed to on their own."

Top tips

- Understand the police core competencies and be able to recite them word for word.

SAMPLE QUESTION NUMBER 4

If one of the members of your team was gay and they told you this over a cup of tea at work, how do you think you would react?

Sample response

"I would have no problem at all. A person's sexual preference is their right and they should not be treated any differently for this. My attitude towards them and our working relationship would not be affected in any way. I have always treated everyone with respect and dignity at all times and will continue to do so throughout my career."

Top tips

* Understand everything there is to know about equality and fairness. If you do not believe in it then this job is not for you.

* Visit the website www.gay.police.uk.

SAMPLE QUESTION NUMBER 5

If you were given an order that you thought was incorrect would you carry it out?

Sample response

"Yes I would. I would always respect my senior officers and their decisions.

However, if I thought something could be done in a better way then I do think that it is important to put it across, but in a structured and non-confrontational manner. During a debrief would probably be an appropriate time to offer up my views and opinions if asked but I would never refuse to carry out an order or even question it during an operational incident or otherwise."

SAMPLE QUESTION NUMBER 6

What do you understand by the term equality and fairness?

Sample response

"It is an unfortunate fact that certain groups in society are still more likely to suffer from unfair treatment and discrimination. It is important for the Police Service and its staff to strive to eliminate all forms of unfair treatment and discrimination on the grounds that are specified in their policies or codes of practice.

Equality and fairness is the working culture in which fair treatment of all is the norm."

Top tips

- Try to read the Police Service's policy on equality and fairness. You may be able to find this by visiting their website or asking them for a copy of it to help you in your preparation.

- Consider reading the Race Relations Act, and understand the duties that are placed upon public sector organisations such as the police.

SAMPLE QUESTION NUMBER 7

How do you think the police could recruit more people from ethnic minority groups?

Sample response

"To begin with it is important that Police Services continue to build effective public relations. This can be achieved through certain avenues such as the service's website or even the local press. If the Police Service has a community liaison officer then this would be a good way to break down any barriers in the communities that we want to recruit from.

Another option is to ask people from these specific groups how they view this Police Service and what they think we could do to recruit more people from their community. Along with this it may be an option to focus media campaigns where there are higher populations of ethnic minority groups."

COMPREHENSIVE LIST OF INTERVIEW QUESTIONS TO PREPARE FOR

Q. Why do you want to become a police officer?

Q. What are your strengths?

Q. What are your weaknesses?

Q. What can you tell us about this particular Police Service?

Q. What do you understand by the term 'teamwork'?

Q. What makes an effective team?

Q. Why would you make a good police officer?

Q. What do you think the role of a police officer entails?

Q. If you saw a colleague being bullied or harassed, what would you do?

Q. What do you think the qualities of an effective police officer are?

Q. If one of your colleagues told you that they were gay, how would you react?

Q. What have you done so far to find out about the role of a police officer?

Q. Why do you want to join this particular Police Service?

Q. Give examples of when you have had to work as a team.

Q. What would you do if a member of your team was not pulling their weight or doing their job effectively?

Q. Have you ever had to diffuse a confrontational situation? What did you do and what did you say?

Q. What are the main issues affecting the police at this current time?

Q. What do you understand about the term 'equality and fairness'?

Q. What do you understand by the term 'equal opportunities'?

Q. If you ever heard a racist or sexist remark, what would you do?

Q. Would you say that you are a motivated person?

Q. How do you keep yourself motivated?

Q. Have you ever had to work as part of a team to achieve a common goal?

Q. If you were in the canteen at work and two senior officers began to make homophobic comments, what would you do?

Q. Have you ever made a poor decision? If so, what was it?

Q. If you were ever given an order that you thought was incorrect what would you do?

Q. Have you ever had to work with somebody that you dislike?

Q. What is wrong with your current job? Why do you want to leave it to become a police officer?

Q. Have you ever carried out a project from beginning to end?

Q. How do you think you would cope with the anti-social working hours?

Q. Have you ever had to work shifts?

Q. How do you think you would cope with working the police shift system?

FURTHER TIPS AND ADVICE FOR PREPARING FOR THE FINAL INTERVIEW

- The Police may ask you more generic questions relating to your past experiences or skills. These may be in relation to solving problems, working as an effective team member, dealing with difficult or aggressive people and diffusing confrontational situations. Make sure you have examples for each of these.

- Try to speak to current serving police officers of the service that you are applying to join. Ask them what it is like to work for that particular constabulary and what the current policing issues are. From their feedback take the positive points but don't use any detrimental or negative feedback during the interview.

- Try to think of a time when you have made a mistake and how you learnt from the experience.

- Don't be afraid to ask the interviewer to repeat a question if you do not hear it the first time. Take your time when answering and be measured in your responses.

- If you don't know the answer to a question then be honest and just say 'I don't know'. This is far better than trying to answer a question that you have no knowledge about. Conversely, if your answer to a question is challenged there is nothing wrong with sticking to your point but make sure you acknowledge the interviewer's thoughts or views. Be polite and never get into a debate.

- You will be scored against the current police core competencies so make sure you try to structure your answers accordingly. The police core competencies are the first thing you should learn during your preparation.

FREQUENTLY ASKED QUESTIONS RELATING TO THE FINAL INTERVIEW

Q. How long will my interview last?

A. Of course, this very much depends on how long your responses are. Generally the interview will last between 45 and 60 minutes.

Top tips

- Make sure you drink plenty of water the day before the interview. This will help your mind to stay focused and also keep you hydrated during your interview.

- Avoid alcohol the day before the interview and certainly do not have a drink the day of the interview. Whilst this may help to calm your nerves, the panel will be able to smell alcohol on your breath.

Q. Do you think I should ask questions at the end of my interview?

A. This can't do any harm providing that the questions aren't inappropriate or harmful to your chances of success. Questions such as "Thank you for taking the time to interview me, can you tell me what the next stage is please?" are satisfactory questions.

However, questions such as "I have read that the Police Service in this area have been criticised for their poor crime reduction figures lately, what are they going to do about it?" are definitely not advised. Do not try to be clever!

Top tips

- Be smart. Tidy hair, clean shoes, suit etc all create a good image.

- Also spend time sitting upright in a chair at home and pretend that you are being interviewed.

- Carry out a mock interview prior to your actual interview day.

- When answering your questions respond to the panel as opposed to the person who has asked you the question.

- Make eye contact with the members of the panel as opposed to looking at the floor. However, don't be aggressive in your eye contact.

Q. Is it okay to use 'body language' during my interview to express myself?

A. Yes, most definitely.

Using your hands or facial expression during any interview is a positive aspect as it demonstrates confidence. However, there is a fine line between subtle expression and overdoing it. If it becomes too obvious then it can be off-putting for the panel. Try sitting in front of a mirror and practice saying the reasons why you want to become a police officer. This will give you an idea of what the panel will be looking at during your interview.

Top tips

- Sit upright in the chair at all times and do not slouch.

- Smile whenever possible and be confident.

- Rest the palms of your hands on your knees when you are not using them to express yourself and keep your feet flat on the ground.

Q. What are the scoring criteria for the final police officer interview?

A. Don't get tied down or concerned with specific pass marks or pass rates.

The police will score you using their own criteria. Where possible, try to structure your responses to the interview questions around the core competencies.

You may find some of the following phrases useful when constructing your answers:

- Dignity and respect;
- Team working and working with others;
- Strong working relationships;
- Effective team member;
- Achieving common goals;
- Customer focus;
- Public service;
- Resilient;
- Community policing;
- Sensitive to cultural issues;
- Sensitive towards racial differences;
- Presenting the right image to the public;

- Effective communication;

- Identify problems and make effective decisions;

- Motivated, conscientious and committed;

- Calm, considerate and can work well under pressure.

CHAPTER 7

Police Officer Interview

Update 2016

The police have now introduced sweeping changes to the interview process. Although the 20 minute interview board will still consist of 4 questions, now 2 of these questions will examine your values and motivations for wanting to join the service, and how these match with the police officer expectations; and the other 2 will test your knowledge of the core competencies. To 'It's important to note that all 4 questions will test your application of all of the competencies, and not just the 2 competency based questions.

You will be given 5 minutes per question, and will be stopped if your answer goes over 5 minutes. In order to help generate a comprehensive response, you could be asked further questions based on your answer.

In your answers, you will be assessed against how well you match the type of behaviours needed to work as a police officer. To recap, these behaviours/core competencies are as follows:

- Decision Making
- Professionalism
- Service Delivery
- Serving The Public
- Working With Others
- Openness To Change

What all of this means is that you will need to prepare more thorough answers to the questions that you will be asked. Below we've included two sample questions from the first half of the interview, where the assessors will try to gage your motivations for joining the service. The final interview questions that we provided you with in the previous chapter will be a great starting point from which you can create your response.

Take a look at the sample questions below.

SAMPLE QUESTION 1

What is it that makes working in the Police Service an attractive career for you?

In this question, the assessors are looking to gage your knowledge of the role, in order to ascertain how well you understand the competencies required. Why do you want to work in the Police Service, does not simply mean 'give the reasons you want to work here'. It means that the reasons you give for wanting to work in the police should interlink with what the police actually do on a regular basis. For example, don't just say I want to work for the police because I want to deter criminals. Tell the assessors that you want to work for the police because I want to deter criminals, and in doing so provide a great service to the general public.

Try to construct your own answer to this question in the box below, and then compare it with our sample response.

Sample Response:

From a very early age, I have been interested in joining the Police Service. My late Father was a high ranking officer and it is from him that I picked up a wealth of knowledge and respect for the way in which the police operate. Firstly I am hugely impressed by the way in which the police go about protecting and safeguarding the public. I know that the primary duty of the police is to serve the welfare of the general public, and this is very important to me, as I have worked in customer service roles for most of my career.

Secondly I am hugely enthusiastic about working as part of a dedicated team, to resolve criminal matters. I know that teamwork is vitally important for police officers, who must work in coordination with the other members of their unit and senior instruction at all times. This organised and disciplined approach is extremely appealing to me, and I believe I'd work extremely well under these conditions.

Another fundamental reason that I have applied to join the Police Service, is the professionalism and decency that members of the service demonstrate on a regular basis. Throughout my life I have always tried to abide by a strong and fair code of ethics, and I believe that the Police Service mirrors these principles. I would love the chance to use my ethical values in professional practice, and as such, working in the police presents the ideal career for me.

Finally, I'm attracted to the challenges that working in the police would present me with. I know that working for the police requires great decision making, conviction and courage, and I believe I am someone who can fully demonstrate all of these qualities. Protecting the public is no easy job, but by taking responsibility and acting in line with the core police values, we really can make a difference to other people's lives.

SAMPLE QUESTION 2

Why do you think that you would make a good police officer?

In this question, the assessors are looking for you to (broadly) show that you are in possession of the qualities required to become a police officer. You'll be given a chance to demonstrate **how** you have used these competencies in the next 2 questions, but in this question you are essentially being asked to identify that you have the competencies required, and why they are important for police officers. For example, don't just tell the assessor that you are a great team player. Tell the assessor that you are a great team player and that you know this will help you in the Police Service, as officers have to work as part of a disciplined and organised unit. Then, provide an example of when you have used teamwork in the past.

Try to construct your own answer to this question in the box below, and then compare it with our sample response.

Sample Response:

There are a number of reasons why I believe that I would be a great fit for the Police Service:

Firstly, I am someone with excellent public service skills. I have worked in the public sector for most of my life, dealing first-hand with customers, and therefore I am extremely well versed in communicating and assisting members of the public. I know that this is an essential skill for police officers to have, as their primary role is to serve and protect the community around them. My customer service roles have ensured that I have impeccable skills in service delivery/delivering a great service to customers. This is a quality which is extremely important for police officers, as it is vital that the public can maintain their faith in the service.

Secondly, I believe that I am someone who strongly demonstrates the ethical principles of the Police Service, in particular – professionalism. At all times, I strive to work as ethically and professionally as possible. I am a polite, fair and considerate person who always takes the sensible course of action. I know that this is essential for the Police Service, as officers of the police are role models in society, and therefore must always strive to set a good example.

Thirdly, I believe that as a result of working in leadership roles throughout my career, I am someone who can make difficult decisions with relative ease. I have often been placed in positions where a firm judgement was needed in order to resolve a situation, and have absolutely no problem in making these decisions if necessary. I know that this is an important part of police work. Officers are expected to take responsibility for their actions and make safe and responsible decisions, which will benefit their colleagues' safety, public safety and their own safety.

I also believe that I have fantastic team working skills. I have worked as a leading member of many teams in my career, and therefore I am no stranger to this discipline. Working as part of a team involves discipline, coordination and cooperation, and I'm hugely impressed with the way that the Police Service goes about handling this. Crime cannot be handled by one person alone, it takes a whole team of individuals working in unison, and that is why it is important for police to work as a larger unit. To add to this, I'm very adaptable, and believe that I could be placed into any team, gel and produce outstanding work. This is important, as I know that I could be asked to work with a wide range of different people when working for the police, both inside and outside of the service.

Competency Based Questions

You have now arrived at the 2 core competency based questions. In these questions, you will be tested on your ability to demonstrate that you understand the core competencies, and that you have used them in the past.

In your responses, you should try to demonstrate as many of the core competencies as you can. By the end of your fourth answer, you must have fully demonstrated all 6. While you won't be penalised for repeating any of the competencies, you should try to spread them out across all 4 questions, whilst still making sure that you answer each question to the best of your ability.

SAMPLE QUESTION 3

Can you give me an example of where you have dealt with a difficult situation in your professional life?

Sample Response

During my time as an administrator, I was often required to make difficult decisions. One such occasion that I can remember was when a member of my team turned up to work in an inebriated state. The individual in question had undergone severe personal trauma. While he had been offered time off to deal with this, he refused. Some of the other members of the management team felt that the best course of action was to send him home and release him from the company. They were uncomfortable with his behaviour and believed that, because he refused to take time off, attending the office in this state was extremely unprofessional. I was ultimately tasked with making the decision on what to do with the employee.

My first decision was what to do with the employee on an immediate basis. While I would certainly be sending him home, I decided that my options were a) to call the police, b) to assign someone from the office to take him home, or c) to use a contact number for someone to collect him and take him home. I decided upon option C. While there were a number of willing volunteers, I did not want to further damage the day's work. A relative of the employee arrived swiftly and took him home in her car.

My second decision was whether the employee should be sacked. I weighed up all of the options before making this decision. If we fired him, we would be showing a lack of sensitivity and understanding as a company. If we did not fire him, we might be setting a bad example. I ultimately decided that I was prepared to give him one final chance, since this was the first time it had happened. The individual in question was a very capable employee and losing him would only damage the business.

I called the employee the next morning, and spoke to him about the situation. I informed him in a sensitive manner that if he wished to keep his job, then he a) needed to take some time off to deal with his issue, and b) needed to use this time to seek therapy or guidance. I reassured him that the company would support him through this difficult period in his life.

The end result of this situation was that the employee took a two week break, and came back feeling better. He is still at the company, and has now risen to a management position. I believe that by making measured decisions, I ultimately aided the company long term.

SAMPLE QUESTION 4

Can you give me an example of when you have successfully managed a project or task?

Sample Response

When I was working in my previous position as an administrator, I was required to work in teams on a daily basis. Often, I was positioned as the leader of these teams. On one occasion that I can remember, our task was to organise a company-

wide event. This would involve hiring out independent entertainment workers, food suppliers, health and safety specialists and other essential staff. I was one of three sub-leaders of the team, and had around 30 people under my command.

My main priority was finding the relevant healthy and safety staff. I did this because health and safety at such an event should be a top priority. It is the responsibility of the company to ensure that they have met recognised safety standards, and to maintain the wellbeing of all attendees at their event. In the event of an injury, a failure to implement health and safety procedures could seriously damage the business. I made contact with the paramedical department of the local hospital, and requested if they could free up several members of staff and at least two vehicles, for the day of the event.

I then liaised with both of the other team leaders, to ensure that I had all of the details of exactly what they were planning. I paid particular attention to the entertainments organiser. Between us, we worked out exactly which health and safety procedures would need to be put in place to accommodate the activities being arranged.

Following this meeting, I instructed the team under my control to make contact with the local fire service, and the local Police Service, and request for staff members from each sector to be available on the day of the event. We successfully negotiated a time and fee.

The event was a tremendous success and there were no serious injuries to report. At the end of the event, I was congratulated by my boss on my efforts in securing the participation of these crucial safety management services.

CHAPTER 8

The Police Officer fitness test

The fitness test stage of the police selection process covers two specific areas.

These are as follows:

- The Endurance Test or Multi Stage Fitness Test;
- The Dynamic Strength Test.

On the following pages I have provided you with information relating to each of the two individual sections but it is important that you check with the service you are applying to join that the information is correct.

The police fitness test is not too difficult but obviously this will very much depend on your own abilities. With a degree of focused preparation you can pass the police fitness test with relative ease. Use the 'How to get Police Officer fit' information guide during your preparation.

You may also wish to purchase the actual endurance test/ bleep test audio CD from our online shop how2become.com. This CD is a very similar to the test used by the police and you will find it a useful tool in your preparation.

THE ENDURANCE TEST

The endurance test, also known as the 'multi-stage fitness test', 'bleep' or 'shuttle run' test, is often used by sports coaches and trainers to estimate an athlete's VO2 Max (maximum oxygen uptake). Apart from the police, the test is also used by the Armed Forces, Emergency Services and Prison Service as part of their selection process but it is also a great way to improve and monitor your own fitness level.

Description
The 'bleep' test involves running continuously between two

points that are 15 metres apart (20 metres in some cases). These 'shuttle' runs are done in time to pre-recorded 'bleep' sounds on an audio CD or cassette. The time between the recorded 'bleeps' decreases after each minute and therefore the test becomes progressively harder with each level completed. The full test consists of approximately 23 levels but the actual police endurance test only requires you to achieve 4 shuttles at level 5 to pass. Each level lasts approximately 60 seconds.

A level is basically a series of 15 metre 'shuttle runs'. The starting speed is normally 8.5 km/hr, which then increases by 0.5km/hr with each new level.

To purchase your copy of the bleep test please visit www.how2become.com.

THE DYNAMIC STRENGTH TEST

This test mimics a seated bench press action and a seated rowing action. You will be asked to perform 5 repetitions on both the push and pull aspects. The machine works out the average of your 5 repetitions and gives you a score. You must push 34kg and pull 35kg to pass.

Two of the most effective ways to prepare for this type of test include rowing (using a rowing machine) and press ups. The reason why I recommend rowing during your preparation is that apart from increasing your physical strength it will also help prepare you for the endurance test.

IMPORTANT: Make sure you consult a medical practitioner prior to engaging in any strenuous physical exercise program.

A FEW FINAL WORDS

You have now reached the end of the guide and no doubt you will be ready to start preparing for the police officer selection process. Just before you go off and start on your preparation, consider the following.

The majority of candidates who pass the police officer selection process have a number of common attributes. These are as follows:

1. They believe in themselves.

The first factor is self-belief. Regardless of what anyone tells you, you can become a police officer. Just like any job of this nature, you have to be prepared to work hard in order to be successful. Make sure you have the self-belief to pass the selection process and fill your mind with positive thoughts.

2. They prepare fully.

The second factor is preparation. Those people who achieve in life prepare fully for every eventuality and that is what you must do when you apply to become a police officer. Work very hard and especially concentrate on your weak areas.

3. They persevere.

Perseverance is a fantastic word. Everybody comes across obstacles or setbacks in their life, but it is what you do about those setbacks that is important. If you fail at something, then ask yourself 'why' you have failed. This will allow you to improve for next time and if you keep improving and trying, success will eventually follow. Apply this same method of thinking when you apply to become a police officer.

4. They are self-motivated.

How much do you want this job? Do you want it, or do you really want it?

When you apply to join the police you should want it more than anything in the world. Your levels of self-motivation will shine through on your application and during your interview. For the weeks and months leading up to the police officer selection process, be motivated as best you can and always keep your fitness levels up as this will serve to increase your levels of motivation.

Work hard, stay focused and be what you want...

Richard McMunn

Richard McMunn